In Demand

How to Get Hired, Develop Your Career and Always be Successful

Bill Van Steenis

with Greg Smith

Black Lake Press

TELL YOUR STORY
BLACKLAKEPRESS.COM

Black Lake Press

TELL YOUR STORY
BLACKLAKEPRESS.COM

Cover design by Greg Smith of Black Lake Studio.

Published by Black Lake Press of Holland, Michigan.
Black Lake Press is a division of Black Lake Studio, LLC.
Direct inquiries to Black Lake Press at *www.blacklakepress.com.*

ISBN 978-0-9824446-1-0

For my wonderful wife Barbara who is my friend and my life partner and for our lovely daughter Jennifer. Barb, you and I have been through a lot together these many years, some good and some not so good but always worth the trip. Thanks for your love and support and for having enough faith for both of us when mine runs low. Jen, thanks for your jokes, your crazy sense of humor, and your unwavering love. I have the two best girls any guy could ask for.

Acknowledgments

I have many people to thank who have believed in me and helped me through this process.

My daughter Jennifer and my son-in-law Kyle Ross are a never-ending source of encouragement to me. I am so grateful to have you in my life.

My parents Ross and Betty van Steenis have taught me much. My dad taught me the value of work and the importance of doing everything with excellence. He also taught me the importance of valuing and protecting my personal reputation. My mother Betty has loved and encouraged me all my life and stood by me and believed in me as only a mother can believe in a son. For that love and support I will be forever grateful. Thanks Mom.

My business partner and sister-in-law Angela Schut has been a great friend and supporter. Angela has forced me to learn to think before I speak....most of the time. Thank you Angela for your thousands of hours of working side by side with me for the same common goal, to always deliver our clients more than they expected and to make everyone we come in contact with feel better about themselves than when they met us.

My dear friend and co-author Greg Smith did a masterful job of weaving my thoughts and ideas together in a cohesive work that has become *In Demand* and *The ReExamined Life*. Without Greg's extraordinary skills, hard work and dedication to this project it would not have been possible. Thanks, Greg, for your vision and dedication to this work. I'm looking forward to our next book together.

Dr. Dale Van Steenis has been my friend and mentor as well as an important member of my family. We are closer than brothers and have traveled the world together for a cause much greater than our own, to touch the hearts of people for Christ.

Bob Walker has been my closest of friends and partner in crime and many other adventures for more than forty-five years. You've kept me out of more trouble than I want to think about. Everyone needs a friend like you Bob. Thanks for being there my friend.

Doyle Passmore has been my very close friend and spiritual accountability partner for nearly two decades. Doyle, you've seen me through the good times and the bad, the times of blessing and the times of trial. We are brothers in Christ and friends for life. You have always encouraged me and stood by me when I needed someone who would tell me the truth. I can't tell you how much I appreciate your honesty, your encouragement and your loyalty.

Rob Stam of The Big Red Group (www.bigredgroup.com)

is my friend and publicist. Rob has worked tirelessly to make sure I have received high quality publicity. He is relentless in his work on my behalf. Thanks Rob for all your help.

In life we all have our heroes. My hero is a man named Ephraim Lindor. Ephraim heads up El Shaddi Ministries in Port-au-Prince, Haiti, where he pastors a church of more than 400 people while working full time as a communications specialist for Compassion International. He is one of the bravest and most generous men I have ever known. On January 12, 2010 a 7.0 earthquake devastated Port-au-Prince, Haiti. I was frantic trying to learn if my friend had survived the quake. At 3:47 AM I heard a ping on my cell phone letting me know I had received a text message. It was Ephraim, "Brother! Taliana (his daughter) and I escape by a miracle. I was at the Montana when it collapsed. We are safe but food in the black market remains a challenge as I shelter many people." I prayed a prayer of gratitude to God for sparing my dear friend and his family. Ephraim went without sleep and very little food for several days as he searched for friends and church members. He sheltered more than twenty-five people for days at his home and many more at his church, making sure they were fed and that their medical needs were taken care of. During all of this I never heard a single word of discouragement, self-pity or negativity. This man is the most selfless man I have ever known and a hero among men.

I have probably learned more about the value of humility and sacrifice from Ephraim than from any other person with the exception of Jesus Christ. Bless you my friend. You are an inspiration to me.

Dr. Tom Stout has been both my dear friend and my partner in ministry in Haiti. Thanks Tom for your friendship and for your kindness and your unending generosity in our shared ministry in Port-au-Prince.

Doctors Sean Growney and Diane Bigham and my good friend Erin Lamb, MS, PT keep me going. Without your help and your wise counsel I would not have been able to do this project. In fact, I wouldn't be doing anything. Thanks for your friendship and your outstanding care.

Dorothy Plummer has been a wonderful friend and more than that a second mom to Barb and me for nearly thirty years. She is more than 90 years young and inspires me to be a better person every time I talk with her. Thanks Mom.

As special thanks to the many family, friends, colleagues and professionals who contributed greatly to the content of this book. Richard Gwynn, Denise Dorigo-Jones, Kevin McMahon, Tim Gargaro, Phil Damaska, Reeder Singler, Curt Arnold, Kevin Comer, Bill Whalen, Craig Barnhart, Bruce Los, Cory Beuerle, Jeff Bonebrake, John Zarb, Jon van Steenis, Regan van Steenis, Ryan van Steenis, Kyle Luke, Lauren Anderson, Barbara Yandell, Patty Baer, Jerry Nienhuis, Sheldon Stone, Steve Pennington, and any others whom I failed to mention.

Finally and most important I thank God my Father for the inspiration for this book and the strength to write it. I thank His Son, my Lord and Savior Jesus Christ for loving me when I was unlovable and for being willing to endure the horror of the cross for the sake of a single soul.

I am honored that you chose my book. I hope you find that you are both challenged and encouraged through the reading of this book. I pray for your success.

Bill van Steenis
January 21, 2010

Contents

Introduction:

Welcome to Earth

This is not a book about the way things ought to be. It's about the way things are.

We spend too much time and energy arguing about the way the world should be. Each of us thinks that we know what the government ought to do, how businesses ought to operate, how consumers ought to spend their money. Our family, religion, politics and education all shape our sense of right and wrong, and most of us try to make the world a better place, in some way. This is a good thing: a vision of and a commitment to justice is part of what makes us human. Think of what life would be like if no one cared.

Unless we also pay attention to the way the world actually is, not just the way we think that it should be, we can make ourselves miserable. Imagine someone living in a valley, near a river. As the river rises he tells his neighbors that the government should have built a dam up the valley years ago. As it overflows its banks, he shouts at his neighbors (as they flee the area) that they ought to stay and put up sandbags. As he sits on his roof, surrounded by the flood, he shakes his fist at the military helicopters, demanding a rescue. My point is that while we ought to strive for a better world, we also need to be shrewd enough to survive in the real one.

This book is about approaching our careers with that kind of realism. Specifically, it's whether you will get hired when you apply for a job, kept on when there are layoffs and promoted when there's an opening above you. If you're self-employed, it determines whether you will get enough work, at a high enough rate, to survive and thrive. It's also about whether you will set the pace and the terms in your career, or be dependent on someone else's generosity, desperation or favors.

This entire book is based on a key insight about how the world really works: if you have something that people want and need badly enough, they will pay you for it. The more they want and need it, the more they will pay for it. That's called demand. If enough people want and need something, other people will find a way to sell it to them. That's called supply. The more supply that exists, the lower the price people will pay: as the old joke goes, it's hard to sell snowballs to Eskimos. This is the Law of Supply and Demand. In your career, you want to sell yourself (I mean your time, skills, services, etc.) for as much as possible. You want them to hire you, pay you and promote you. For that to happen two things need to be true. First, what you offer must be *in demand*: it has to be something that people really want and need. Second, what you offer must be unique enough that they will pay you, instead of (and hopefully more than) someone else for it.

Let me give you a popular example of how our focusing on who should be in demand and what they ought to get paid clouds our understanding of how the job market really works. Repeatedly I've heard someone make the point that it's unfair that professional athletes make millions of dollars for hitting a ball, while schoolteachers earn a middle class income. Their point is that because teachers are so important to society they should make more than ballplayers.

Of course everyone recognizes that education is more important than baseball, but tens of thousands of people will buy tickets to watch someone hit home runs, while no one will buy tickets to watch someone teach fourth grade. Hitting home runs in major league stadiums is rare and entertaining enough that many people will pay a relatively small amount—the price of a ticket—to see it. On the other hand, there are perhaps 100,000 fourth grade teachers in the United States (I just found a government statistic online that said there were 90,000+ elementary schools in America, and I'm guessing that the average school has at least one-fourth grade teacher). There's too much supply and not enough demand for any one teacher to get a multimillion dollar contract. Every parent, and I think every citizen, is grateful for dedicated teachers. That demand doesn't mean that there's a paying audience to watch spelling tests.

The "should" and "ought to" arguments block our view of the way things are. Should teachers get raises? Should factory workers have their jobs and wages protected by union, or government rules? The nurse in the hospital was nicer and seemed more on-the-ball than the surgeon that spoke to you for only a couple of minutes: shouldn't the nurse make as much as the surgeon? The available supply of teachers, factory workers and nurses, relative to the demand, determines their job security and pay. The available supply of Sports Illustrated swimsuit models and orthopedic surgeons is lower, relative to the demand for them, and so they have greater security and pay. It's not about justice, it's about the laws of supply and demand.

Welcome to Earth. You can grumble that it's not fair, you can vote for politicians who promise to change the system, you can go through life frustrated because you don't get hired or promoted or paid enough. You can do all those things, but they won't do you any good. On the other hand, you can understand the market and the demand for what you have to offer and provide it better than your competitors. If you do that, you will be in demand, at least within your field, industry, area or however your marketplace is defined.

Let me clear up three potential misunderstandings right now. First, I'm not saying that you should go through life always trying to make as much money as possible. You may want to teach fourth grade. You may love it, other people love you for it, and you know that you're doing something valuable with your life that brings joy and changes lives. Please don't stop doing that! If that's the case, don't you want to be in demand as a teacher? To have your choice of schools, or to have the administration, parents and students support you fully? If you apply for a new position, don't you want to get it? Being in demand means that you will be recognized as not only a member of a valuable profession, but as a valuable member of that profession. Second, not all of us can choose to be equally in demand, just as everyone can't be above average. The world is a competitive place, whether we think it should be or not. Finally, I'm not saying that we shouldn't strive for justice in the economy or the workplace. Some people are not in demand for unjust reasons, such as racism or favoritism. We should not tolerate playing fields that aren't level.

And yet, all other things being equal, we need to recognize that some people can offer skills or services better, cheaper or faster than others, and those people are always going to be more in demand than those that can't. Welcome to Earth.

This book is about understanding what makes some people in demand throughout their career. It's not so much about the opposite: I'm going to spend more time talking about what succeeds than what fails. The book is divided into four sections. In the first section I'm going to help you figure out how the job market really works. In the second section I'm going to tell you what to do to make yourself marketable. In the third section I'll give you some keys to selling yourself to the people who hire or buy from you, and in the final section I'm going to share some advise about staying in demand throughout your career.

You might wonder what I know about this subject, and why you should take my advice. I don't have a PhD in economics, nor am I a tycoon who has run industries. For almost twenty-five years I've been a career recruiter, owning a company that matched men and women with available jobs all around the world. I've seen, up close and personal, why and how some people get hired, retained or promoted and why others don't. I've had companies that rejected every candidate that I brought to them, and had to figure out why. I've also had candidates that I couldn't buy a job for, and had to figure out why. In my last book, *The ReExamined Life: Finding a Better Life After Losing a Job* (2009, Black Lake Press) I looked at how to rebuild a career after getting laid off, particularly in a recession when the job market is tight. People who read that book said that they wished someone had given them this advice before they lost their job. I heard from employers who told me how much easier it would be for them, and their employees, if young people coming out of school understood how the job market really works. Out of that feedback, this book was born. I hope that it helps you to become in demand.

Section I:
"How the World Works"

Chapter 1:
In Demand or Just Demanding?

When I was 35 years old, I went to work for an accounting firm. At the time, I really needed a job.

When I got the offer I was high as a kite. My wife and I went over the offer letter, excited about the salary package and the benefits. We talked excitedly about where we would live. I fantasized about my office, about my perks and about what the rhythm of my working week would be like. It was a real answer to prayer, and we rejoiced about how this would solve so many of our problems.

On my first day on the job I walked in with a spring in my step and a grin on my face. I shook everyone's hand, hung my coat and got settled into my corner office. I allowed myself to lean back in my new chair for a moment and feel content. This job was going to take care of me and my family.

I'd been sitting there not five minutes, basking in a warm,

secure glow, when one of the partners walked in and handed me a form. It was an IRS form to extend the tax return of one of the firm's clients. I looked at it, confused. I didn't think that I'd be handling much tax work. I had been trained in forensic accounting and litigation work. That's what I wanted to do, and assumed that they would want to use me for those types of cases. I honestly had no idea how to fill out this form that was in my hands.

It didn't take me long to realize that my new employer didn't care what I wanted to work on. My wants, needs, desires and problems were the furthest thing from their mind. I quickly dawned on me that they had hired me to solve their problems, not mine. They were overwhelmed with public accounting clients. Tax returns were stacking up and needed to be filed. That's what needed to be done. When I tried to gently point out that I had hoped they would let me work on litigation cases they stared. I could almost hear crickets chirping. They patiently explained, as if they were talking to a child, that they didn't have enough litigation work to allow me to focus on that. What they did have was a giant and ever-growing-bigger stack of tax work that needed to be handled as quickly as possible. I pleaded, and tried to bargain with them to let me start a litigation department. They stared at me like I had just said that I wanted to build a racquetball court in the office and organize an employee tournament.

I lasted eight months with that firm, the longest eight months of my life.

Along the way I learned a valuable lesson: employers hire employees to solve the employer's problem, not the employee's. The same thing is true with consumers: they buy from vendors or hire contractors to fill their wants and needs, not the wants and needs of the seller.

Talking to people over the years, I'm convinced that we've all had a moment like this: we took a job because it was a good deal for us. We were so focused on how the job was going to solve our problems, on what the employer was going to do for us and our family, that we didn't think too much about what the employer needed and wanted from us. We walked in, excited to fill out the employment papers and bring the benefits folder home to our spouse. Our head was full of all the things that we wanted to do and achieve in our new workplace. Then reality hit: we had been hired for something we couldn't do, or didn't want to do. When we realized that we were a square peg in a round hole we tried to change the shape of the hole: we argued about our job description, we focused on what interested us and ignored what didn't or tried to move to a different position inside the company. We were frustrated or discouraged because our employer didn't seem to care what we wanted or needed.

Of course they didn't. That's not why they hired us. Companies hire people to solve the company's problems, not the other way around.

Friends who are self-employed have had these moments as well: the signed bid and the deposit check felt great. Then they started the project and realized that the client expected something different from what the contractor was prepared to give. They began to wonder what they had gotten themselves into and why they had agreed to this deal in the first place. We've all been on the consumer side of that: when we buy a good or a service, anything from a car to a haircut, it never occurs to us to base our purchase on what the manufacturer, salesperson, stylist or salon want and need. We give them money so that they will solve our problems, not theirs.

If you need a job, here's my question: what will you do to get it? Are you prepared to focus on the problems, desires and expectations of the person who hires you? Or are you looking for someone to help you out by paying your bills while you pursue your own interests?

It's OK to be honest. Be honest with yourself, at least. If you're looking for an employer or customer that will give you what you need to solve your problems or fulfill your dreams then acknowledge that to yourself. Be aware that such expectations come with a price: your relationships with employers and customers are probably going to be rocky and short. You will probably be the kind of person who does the minimum required in each situation to move on to the next opportunity. You can try to follow a lonely road to the top by being self-centered and using other people and situations to advance your ambitions. You will probably leave a long line of coworkers and clients feeling used and abused.

There is an alternative, of course: being a person who is *in demand.* Some people are so focused on the wants and needs of employers and customers that they have a line of people bidding for their work or services. They get multiple offers and have a waiting list of clients. They also have a resume or client list full of glowing reviews, and are welcome back anywhere they've ever worked.

People who are in demand have a bigger vision for their work: they realize that it's not about them. They realize employers or customers that give them money deserve to be satisfied, to the best of their ability. They are oriented toward serving the company, the customer or the team. They give people their money's worth in effort and accomplishment.

As a result, In Demand People get their needs met as well. Satisfied clients, customers and employers are happy to pay a fair price for having their needs met. Customers and companies will pay In Demand People whatever it takes, if it's within their means.

So if you work for a company and you make your focus solving the problems of the organization and the people around you, you will have as much job security as that company can give. They won't want to lose you. If you own a business and you put your customers first, genuinely caring about giving them what they paid for, you will always have customers.

On the other hand, if you focus on your own problems, always talk about what you want and need and believe that your job exists to benefit you, you won't be in demand. You will just be demanding.

There is too much of this sort of thinking in the marketplace today. I understand the pain of joblessness or business without enough customers. I've experienced both of those plenty of times in my own career. I feel terrible for workers whose industries have collapsed and who can't find new work. When we talk about how politicians and employers should "create jobs" we ignore the reality that jobs are only created when there are problems that can be solved by hiring people to do that work.

The other day, driving in the car, I listened to a discussion on the radio about how the government ought to create jobs by hiring people to restore historic buildings which are falling into decay. That sounded like a good idea: some people who need money and health insurance would get it, and some historic buildings would get fixed up. Then one of the other people in the discussion pointed out that if those particular old buildings are so important, the government could just contract out the restoration work to experienced construction companies. The first speaker replied by saying that the taxpayers would never approve spending money on these restorations for their own sake. No one really thought that these old buildings were worth the cost of repairing. The point was to create jobs for people who needed them, and since we'd be paying these people anyway, we might as well get something for it, like sprucing up abandoned buildings and the like. So the first speaker's point was that we would hire people, not because there was any problem that was so bad we were willing to spend money to solve it, but rather to create jobs for their own sake.

I've been unemployed, more than once in my life. I sympathize with the plight and the pain of those who don't have a job. Even so, the plan the first person in the radio discussion was floating just won't work, because that's not how the real world functions. Unemployed people shouldn't pin their hopes on government schemes for which there is no legitimate demand. They need to find the real problems that employers and customers are willing to spend money to solve. That may not be the type of work that the unemployed person wants to do, and it may not solve all of their problems. If we begin with that mindset we will be on our way to being in demand.

I have a friend that happens to be a senior vice president of a very large energy company in Texas. I sent Ken a copy of my first book, *The ReExamined Life,* and he read it just before he was scheduled to interview a group of newly graduated accounting students. Ken told me that repeatedly during the hiring process he was asked what he and his company could do for the applicants. What he did not hear is how any of these newly graduated professionals would bring added value to Ken's department or company. Few seemed interested in the problems Ken needed to solve by filling his open positions.

Ken told me that he went back to his office, reread *The ReExamined Life* and decided to hire only two of the forty applicants he interviewed. He told me that none of them seemed to understand the basic dynamic in the employer-employee relationship. He is not alone. I have polled executives and hiring managers across industry lines while working on this book, and they all tell me that today's students and recent graduates have an entitlement mindset.

I'm not saying that you shouldn't try to negotiate the best possible compensation deal for yourself, but you negotiate from a position of strength when people want you badly enough to pay your price. That's being in demand, and the irony is that you become in demand when you are first oriented toward serving the customer or employer.

Chapter 2:
The Problem

I have a friend named David from the nation of Malawi, in Africa. He came to the United States to attend university and graduated at the top of his class with a double major in business and computer science while he worked three part time jobs.

Once David had completed his degree he went out into the job market. He took a job with a well-known temporary accounting agency, which sent him to an insurance company to work for a few days while someone was out on vacation. While he was there the company had a major meltdown of their computerized accounting systems. As David was listening to the staff describing the problem he asked the systems manager if he could help. The manager didn't know what else to do so he showed him the problem. It took the better part of the afternoon but David got the system back up and running. He also found the root cause and corrected it so that it wouldn't happen again.

The president of the insurance company came downstairs to meet David that afternoon. He asked if he could do anything for him in return for his help. David politely but boldly asked the president for a job, which he got on the spot. His career really got started because he was a problem solver when a company was in crisis. David went on to become the internal auditing manager for the insurance company. He was there about a year when he was offered the position of Vice President of Internal Audit for a bank. His income went from $30,000 per year as a temp to more than $100,000 per year as an officer of the bank.

David learned the secret to being in demand: find some problem to which you are the best solution. He had the ability and initiative to show that he could fix an expensive problem and became a valuable solution.

Sometimes an employee or contractor solves a more subtle problem for his boss or customer. I once knew an analyst at a large company who was a marginal performer, at best. He took very little initiative and his ideas weren't especially creative or useful. When it came time to give a major presentation to clients it was usually lower level employees under or around him that did the analysis and prepared the recommendations. These coworkers resented him and couldn't fathom why the executive vice president kept this guy in his position. Some made plays to get his job, going to the vice president and trying to prove that they had written the report or come up with the solution.

There was a piece to the puzzle that they didn't see. The lackluster manager was solving a huge problem for the vice president. The company was based in the Midwest but often did business with partners and clients in New York City. The vice president was a capable person, but he was thoroughly Midwestern: he had gone to a state university, worked his way up through the ranks of small businesses in the Great Lakes region and liked snowmobiling, deer-hunting and backyard barbeque. The lackluster manager, on the other hand, had been a star athlete at a prestigious Ivy League university. He provided cover and credibility to the vice president in midtown Manhattan. When his name was attached to a project, the clients in New York felt comfortable, and when he walked into a presentation they listened to the analysis and recommendations, even if they were largely created by employees with less impressive credentials. He bridged a cultural gap for the vice president and kept the clients happy.

The employees that didn't grasp the problem that he was solving for the company became embittered. They understood that his Ivy League background accounted for his position, but they didn't quite get it. When they made end-runs around him to the vice president, arguing that it was their work that was impressing the people in Manhattan, they didn't realize that giving his job to them wouldn't solve any problems for the vice president. Yes, the junior analyst from a state college in Indiana was sharp as a razor, but she simply wasn't going to keep the investors happy over lunch at the Russian Tea Room. Maybe that's not how the world is supposed to work, but it's the way that it does work. The junior analyst trying to upstage the Ivy Leaguer wasn't a problem-solver for the vice president, and that's why she never got anywhere in her battles with him.

Remember that in very large organizations some problems are local. Solving a problem for a multinational corporation can carry less weight than solving a problem in your own department or for your own manager. I've seen managers protect one of their people during a period of layoffs because that employee solved some particular problem for that particular manager. I once knew a gifted executive who, for whatever reason, had never taken the time to master building spreadsheets with formulas and pivot tables. The company required executives to submit many of these sort of data spreadsheets, but she wasn't very good at it and didn't want to take the time to learn. One of her middle managers was not only skilled at this type of work, she was also willing to "brown-bag" her lunch in a conference room with the executive, correcting formulas and fixing links before the weekly reports went off to corporate headquarters. When budget cuts caused layoffs, guess which of her employees the executive went to bat for? She could reassign responsibilities in the department but she couldn't, or didn't want to, function without the person who spent lunch hours helping her prepare the weekly reports. The others who lost their jobs might have been valuable employees, but they weren't as valuable to the executive.

In school we were rewarded for being knowledgeable, clever and articulate. In a labor union we are rewarded for how many years we've been on the job. In a production facility we are rewarded for speed and efficiency. Yet the smartest person in the room isn't always the one who knows the most about the product or one who knows everyone and everything that's happened in the company over the decades or even the one who has made employee of the month seven times over the last five years. The smartest person in the room is the one who figures out what the most relevant problem is for the group and then fixes it. They are the most valuable player.

If problem solving is the key to getting a job, then why worry about college degrees or certifications? If you can show your value to a manager or an organization, what difference does it make where or even whether you went to college? There are two reasons why education still matters.

First, there are things that you learn at college that are valuable in any workplace. Consider communication skills: employers assume that if you have a college degree you must have demonstrated some ability to write and speak with some competence in order to graduate. In a technology-driven economy where business is globally networked, communication skills are more important than ever before. The ability to explain a problem or answer a question in an email is critical in modern industries of every type. How can a company make sure that a new employee won't make a costly mistake in an email, on the phone, or in reading a report or instructions from a supplier on another continent? College may not guarantee good communication skills, but college graduates are more likely to be able to read, write and speak effectively than those who don't have a degree.

Second, some degrees or certification are evidence of very particular skills. I have a friend who works for a company that builds industrial robots for factory assembly lines. When he was young he started working for the company as a mechanic, servicing the robots. Over the years the control systems have become digitally networked. Servicing them requires programming to correct their actions from a laptop, using several computer languages and coordinating with IT network administrators. John went back to night school and got a two-year degree and several other certifications. A company that is having problems with their robots can be assured that he is qualified to repair their systems.

Some people create more problems than they solve. Don't forget that your cost is defined as not only your salary, benefits and operating budget, but the time it takes to manage you and the impact that you make on other people.

I knew a brilliant engineering manager who turned out a great product and kept per-unit costs down and profits high, but he was considered "high-maintenance." He saw himself as a maverick, as the one person in the organization who could see what was wrong and was brave enough to tell the truth about it, crying out like a prophet in the wilderness. Over time his bosses realized that although he was making a profit for the company by engineering great products, he was costing them more than he was worth in time and anxiety, forcing others to clean up after all the squabbles that he started. As times got more stressful at the company he was let go. He never really understood that he was costing the organization more than he made for it. In the end he wasn't a problem solver, he was just a problem.

How does all of this help you in your job search? More to the point, how do you get to show that you're the smartest person in the room if you can't even get into the room? How do you demonstrate that you're a problem solver when you don't know what a prospective employer's problems are yet?

You can research. Company websites are great resources, as are links to their corporate reports or news articles about them. Take every opportunity to talk with personal contacts, mentors and/or other people knowledgeable about a company or an industry. The more you can learn about the types of problems that a company might have, the more you can tailor your approach to a prospective employer to present yourself as a problem solver.

When you interview, make sure that you highlight how you have solved problems in the past. Instead of just stressing your education and employment history, point out the challenges that you have met over your career. Don't just say that you have an IT network administrator certificate, talk about how you led a department through a system migration and increased productivity.

If you ever get the opportunity to speak with someone in management at the company that you would like to work for, listen to them instead of just talking about yourself. Sometimes they will share concerns and frustrations about their business. If you can think on your feet and have good people skills you might be able to make helpful suggestions. Don't push too hard and come off as if you, an outsider, are telling them how to run their business. Whatever occurs to you has probably also occurred to them and they have probably tried it already. If you can make some perceptive observations and have prudent insights into possible solutions, you have the chance to be seen as someone who can at least help solve their problems. You might come off as the smartest person in the room without being in the room yet.

What will you do to get a job? Will you get a degree, make hundreds of calls and send out dozens of resumes? Will you network relentlessly and be likable? Will you get a new suit, stand in lines, go to job fairs? If so, then good: you have increased your odds of finding a new position. Still, the most important thing that you can do, the "killer app" for job hunting, is to be the solution to someone's problem. Figure that out and you will always have work.

Chapter 3:
Ambition versus Opportunity

We've all met people who seem to have no ambition in their career. Some have other goals in life (quality of family life, spiritual development, hobbies, volunteer work, etc.) and they work just enough to support themselves while they put their effort into the things that matter more to them. Others would like to achieve and earn more with their work but they lack the imagination and drive to do anything about it. The early 20th century entrepreneur J.C. Penney, who built a hugely successful chain of department stores, used to say, "Give me a stock clerk with a goal and I'll show you a man who will make history; show me a man without a goal and I'll show you a stock clerk." Ambition is a powerful quality, and like other powerful things, it can result in great good or great evil in the world, depending on the nature of the ambition and the character of the person consumed by it.

Economies have both supply and demand sides. A farmer that grows wheat is the supply side, all of us that eat bread are the demand side. We buy what we want from those who have it or make it. If there is a kind of economics to life, then ambition is the supply side. It's what we want to give to, or force upon, the world. Opportunity is the demand side: it's what the world wants and needs from us.

In Demand People are especially sensitive to the opportunity side, and make it their ambition to respond to those opportunities. The most successful people I have met have an uncanny instinct for detecting and evaluating opportunities. They see gaps and shortcomings, the frustrations or unfilled expectations of people or businesses. Read a book on entrepreneurship and you realize that many of the greatest products and companies in history were conceived not because someone dreamed up an idea out of nowhere or accidentally spilled a beaker in a lab and discovered some new Wonder Thing, but because someone was trying to solve a problem. Often they went through countless possible solutions before they worked out just the right way to meet that need or fill that want. After that, ambition kicked in as they came up with a plan to sell that solution into the marketplace.

The same can be said for careers. Some people do form an early dream to grow up and be something, a film maker, for example, and work relentlessly at it. Some careers require an early ambition because the education and training is so long and selective and expensive, like surgeons and fighter pilots. One doesn't stumble into being a brain surgeon at 42 years old by responding to an advertisement in the classifieds. Most of us discover and develop our careers as we go along through the opportunities that present themselves, often from unexpected sources.

Focusing too intently on our ambitions (what we want to do) can cause us to miss opportunities (things that need to be done) that are all around us. I've met people who repeat the same career mistakes over and over, or ride a failing business down into bankruptcy, because they stubbornly pursue an ambition while ignoring better opportunities all around them.

Most of us have seen the television show *American Idol,* and we've all watched some variation on this story. Hundreds of contestants are waiting in the lobby of a convention center for their turn to make their dreams a reality. The host of the show, Ryan Seacrest, interviews a young man or woman about their ambitions. They are supremely self-confident. They tell Seacrest that music is their life, that they have prepared for this moment as hard as Rocky trained for that fight. They tell him that, yes, they will be the next "American Idol." Some even go so far as to say that it's really not fair to the other contestants having to go up against someone like them, who is just about already a professional singer. They believe that they are total package of an entertainer, the proverbial "triple threat" who can sing, dance and act (and wrote their own music and designed their own costume as well!).

You know what happens next. The poor, self-deluded soul becomes a national laughingstock as they enter the audition room, where they are put on the spot, forced to drop the posing and dancing and other showmanship and told to just simply carry a tune, on key, for a few seconds without accompaniment.

That's when they get hit with the human 2x4 of reality and truth-telling that is Simon Cowell. It's painful to watch, but often the person who has just humiliated themselves in front of millions has a look of shock and denial on their face as the judges try to talk sense into them. Sometimes they argue and beg: the judges don't understand that they really, really want to be a singer, and if they were just given a chance, etc. After that, they walk back out into the lobby and some dig their hole deeper (the First Rule of Holes: if you're in one, stop digging) by telling Ryan that the judges didn't know what they were talking about, that they are still certain that they are an undiscovered star. Sometimes, at this point, we get a clue as to the source of the problem as their mother comes over and reinforces their fantasies, soothing their bruised ego by telling them that they are a great singer and not to listen to that Simon Cowell fellow. The camera shows them walking out of the building, mom probably on her way to buy them an ice cream.

The problem with ambitions is that sometimes they blind us to reality and cause us to chase fantasies, passing up real opportunities along the way. All of us need some reality checks in our life. We all need someone or something to play the Simon Cowell role, keeping us grounded to reality and helping us to sort out fact from fiction.

We need to form and pursue ambitions and respond to opportunities, but we need to keep straight which is which.

The world would stagnate without ambition. Enough has

been said about the power of dreams to motivate us and carry us through various obstacles that I don't need to say more. Insert here every pep talk or graduation speech that you've ever heard.

What are the limits of ambition? It can, at times, carry us to great heights. It can also send us on a wild goose chase, convince us to waste time or effort or resources and keep us from seeing other options. For every American Idol there are the poor, deluded souls who had no business auditioning or pursuing a musical career. For some, even the money spent on singing lessons could have been better invested.

Some of you are thinking: but what if singing brings someone joy? What if it makes their world a better place? Then of course they should sing: in the shower, to their cat, in the church choir. If learning to sing better makes them happy, then lessons are well worth it. I spend money on fly fishing lessons and I'll never earn a dollar from fishing (quite the opposite!), but I like the process and challenge of learning to do it better. It's fun, and gets me outdoors away from my computer. Yet the people who told those wannabe Idols that they could become professional musicians – much less rock stars – did them no favors.

To be in demand with employers and customers you need to be honest about your ambitions. There's nothing wrong with dusting off that dream that's been sitting on the back shelf since you were a teenager, as long as you ground it in reality and pursue it with hard and smart effort. Take a moment and ask yourself whether there is any demand for your novel or restaurant. Sometimes visionaries and risk takers create demand: when people experience something new they want it, even though they had never known it before. Without that kind of risk-taking there would be no new novelists or restauranteurs. Before you invest money and time into a dream, assess the demand and opportunity for what you want to do and understand the risks that you are taking. I've seen desperate people spend their last dollars going to motivational workshops or buying self-help tapes or signing up for multilevel marketing schemes because they became convinced that they could make big money for very little effort if they just believed in their dreams strongly enough (and bought the workshops and memberships and materials). I have seen people go broke chasing careers that they had no realistic chance of getting based on their skills, experience or the marketplace, when other opportunities were available to them.

Ambition is a wonderful thing. Some people should chase unique dreams and pursue jobs outside their comfort zone, start companies, invent new products, write novels or open restaurants or get small business training or apply for a dream job. Some people should audition for *American Idol*. All of us need to go into new ventures with self-awareness about why we are doing it and what our expectations are. This is an old paradox: there is always the story of some novelist who got 47 rejection letters before publishing a hit, and that keeps hope alive for everyone else. It's a logical fallacy wrapped in dishonesty: all great novelists are misunderstood and got rejections + I'm getting rejections = I'm a great, misunderstood novelist. If God has gifted you to write novels or cook or build furniture, then do that. It doesn't mean that you're going to get published, open a successful restaurant or make a living running your own carpentry shop. Maybe you should go for it, maybe not. My plea is to be honest with yourself about who you are, what your real gifts are and what opportunities are available for you at this time.

Chapter 4:
Evaluating Opportunities

We are surrounded with opportunities. Even when the economy struggles there are needs we could meet, jobs we could take, or businesses we could start. It's not a matter of whether we have opportunities, it's which opportunities should we pursue. One way to filter our choices is to ask whether an opportunity is real or fake, good or bad, and faithful or unfaithful.

There are real opportunities and there are fake ones, which are really not opportunities at all. People have always exploited the needs, hopes and fears of others by presenting "opportunities" which only benefit them. Sometimes this is a criminal act, and there are con artists who prey upon the newly unemployed with offers and promises that seem too good to be real. When something seems too good to be true, it is. If there is even a chance that someone is trying to scam you, run away. Other times it's someone offering something of legitimate value, but it's up to you as the consumer to decide if that value is worth your time or money. There are workshops, job retraining programs and books for the newly unemployed, like my first book, *The ReExamined Life*.

You will hear of "job" opportunities that aren't really just sales programs. They place all the cost and risk on you with the promise that, if you're successful, you can make lots of money. The stories of the very small percentage of people that succeed in these programs are used to lure more people into them. You should be suspicious of these claims. Sometimes they want money up front from you in some form (almost a sure sign that it's a scam), but often it costs you nothing. For the people offering this "opportunity" this is a great deal: if I wanted to sell something, especially something intangible that doesn't require me to ship a product and takes no real expertise to sell, why wouldn't I want a vast army of people, all risking their time and money, spread across the land trying to peddle it? It costs me nothing, and if a couple of them get lucky enough to make a sale I'll send them a few percentage points of commission on the back end. Probably.

The best way to evaluate these "opportunities," unless they are an obvious scam (run away), is to ask someone who is knowledgeable about that industry for their evaluation. I had an unemployed friend approach me just the other day to ask my advice. They had been offered an opportunity to sell a product in an industry that I was very familiar with. After hearing about this "offer" I told them that the industry was saturated with that product at the moment and that prices and profits were being driven down. Also, that the next generation of products would hit soon, leaving anyone unfortunate enough to get into the game late (as the advice-seeker would have been) stranded high and dry, representing an obsolete item. Of course the company offering this commission-only position was eager to sign up representatives that cost them nothing in the hopes of squeaking out a few more dollars at the end of their product's life-cycle. As desperate as this friend was for employment, I told them that they would only waste another couple of months that could have been spent looking for a real job.

There may be other, more personal opportunities presented that you need to sift through the "real or fake?" filter. A friend or relative might think that they have a great idea for a business and want you to go in on it with them; there might be a long-shot opening in a company across the country that will cost you $1,000 for a plane ticket to go for an interview, a degree or certification that you could go back to school to get (with student loans) in the hopes that it will qualify you for some position. There is no easy rule for evaluating whether these opportunities are real or not: each must be tested on a case-by-case basis. I strongly encourage you to seek out as many knowledgeable and mature people around you as possible to give you advice, then listen to them carefully.

There are real opportunities that aren't good opportunities. They meet a legitimate need with a legitimate solution and the people involved are trustworthy, but the potential return on the investment isn't large enough to be worth the risk. In other words, there just isn't enough money to be made in the deal. A few weeks ago a friend of mine was considering buying a local restaurant. The current owner had been only breaking even for the last few years, wanted out and was willing to turn it over if my friend took over the payments on the building and the costs. My friend, who has an eye for opportunities, saw that the restaurant wasn't achieving its potential: the hours it was open didn't track with the clientele it was trying to serve, its menu could be simplified and improved, the idea and marketing could be tweaked. He figured that he could take it over, let his wife run it, and they could take it from a break-even operation to running at least a small profit within a year.

As he laid it out, the key phrase that jumped out at me was "small profit," particularly the word "small." As I listened to his plan I was counting the costs: even though it wouldn't take a big sum of money to buy it, he would be tying up most of his cash flow and energy. His current business would suffer. His wife would be at the restaurant 12 hours a day, straining their marriage. It would be a huge drain on this family. I had no doubt that this was a legitimate opportunity and that they had the brains and work ethic to turn a "small profit" over the next year. As he walked through the numbers, it became clear that this wouldn't be worth it: there were easier ways for this family to earn, or save, that amount of money over the next year. Doing the math, his wife would have been working for about two dollars an hour and endangering the well-being of the family. It was a profitable opportunity, but not profitable enough to be worth it.

It might be worth the personal and financial costs of relocating if it advances your career. Many of us have taken a new position because it opened doors to move up. Sometimes that worked out, sometimes it didn't. In my experience, recruiters rarely tell you that if you take the position you'll could get stuck, with no chance of advancement. They'll almost always dangle the possibility of a better job in the organization once you get inside. They may even believe it. Be careful, because all sorts of things can change once you take the job: the company's profitability, mergers and acquisitions, reorganizations. The executive who made you promises could get canned shortly after you get there and you could be seen as one of "his people" who needs to be purged. If you have an opportunity that isn't so good at face value (because of the position, the relocation costs, etc.) but has the potential to lead to bigger and better things, ask yourself first if it makes good sense to accept the position on its own merits. A bad opportunity that doesn't turn into a good opportunity later is just a bad opportunity.

Suppose you have a real opportunity (it's not an illusion or a scam), and it's a good opportunity (you really will make enough money to be worth the cost). Why wouldn't you take that?

There is one other filter I'd like you to consider: is it faithful to your values? There are things in life that you could get paid lots of money to do that would be obviously illegal or immoral. I'm going to trust that you have enough sense not to seize those "opportunities." What about the more complicated and subtle choices that we have to make when evaluating opportunities to feed our families, especially when our options are limited? What about jobs that might endanger your family's well-being by requiring you to spend too much time away? What about the job that would have you selling a product that in your heart you believe is wasteful or dishonest or wrong? What about a job that subjects you to emotional or verbal abuse? What about a job that would place you in situations that might tempt you in ways that you can't bear to be tempted or compromise your moral reputation?

There are no simple answers and no universal rules for how to evaluate whether an opportunity will be faithful to your values in life. We are all unique, and the seasons and contexts of our lives are so fluid that something that is intolerable at one point is bearable at another. Consider time away from the family. For years my friend Greg spent lots of time traveling for his work. People around him would ask how he and his family coped with that; they couldn't fathom how that would affect their own marriage or children or emotional life. Greg has always answered that when his kids were very small he travelled infrequently and his family developed trust and intimacy. As the kids got older and the travel became more frequent, his family found a sort of rhythm to it and got used to his trips as being normal. They adjusted other aspects of the family's life to compensate. Greg tells people who ask that when he sees soldiers in airports on their way to an eight month (or longer) deployment, he feels that he and his family can learn to adjust to him being gone for eight days. The key has always been that he and his family love and value each other, and despite the adaptations that they have to make for his business, their commitment to each other is unchanging and nonnegotiable. When you are faithful to what you value, you can, like water flowing around an obstacle, find a way to adjust.

Another family might not survive that type of separation. I know too many people whose marriage couldn't take that heavy a travel schedule or whose children became strangers. Usually there were other issues, other conflicts in those relationships and the time away only exacerbated those differences. That doesn't mean that the time away wasn't a contributing factor. Perhaps if they had chosen to be at home more, the relationship could have been preserved. It might have meant taking a lower paying job with less prestige and perks; it might have meant that the whole family had to downsize their lifestyle, but if they really valued the relationship more than the money or status, that would have been the faithful choice to make.

I once worked for a company that took advantage of its customers and suppliers. I'm a person who values professional relationships, a real networker, not just for the advantages they bring but because I really do care about people: knowing them, working with them, serving them. That's why I was so good at my job of recruiting people for companies and building alliances with partner firms. The problem was that once the contract was signed the project would transition to other people in the company who would lie and manipulate to extract every possible cent of profit from it. The clients and partner firms felt abused and resentful. I reached a point where I couldn't take it anymore: I was well-paid but the hurt and angry looks that I got from clients and the hostility that I felt from colleagues at professional events wasn't worth what I was being paid. My opportunities in that company were real and profitable, but they were unfaithful to my values. I couldn't represent that company anymore and still be the person that I wanted to be in the industry.

As you evaluate the employment opportunities around you, please pause long enough to consider whether they will be faithful to what is most important to you. Obviously, you need to keep a roof overhead and food on the table, but when deciding between opportunities, ask yourself which one will most help you to become the person that you want to be. That may not always be the highest-paying job.

Section II:
"Make Yourself
Marketable"

Chapter 5:
Be Competent

I love to cook. I've been an amateur chef for years, and love nothing more than spending a day preparing an elaborate dinner party for friends. Naturally, I'm fascinated by some of the cooking shows on TV. There are two types that especially interest me and are worth talking about in this chapter.

The first type are competitions that pit two or more chefs against each other and the clock to take an assortment of surprise ingredients and create an original dish that impresses a panel of judges.

The second type are restaurant reality shows. My favorite series in the genre features a world-famous chef and restauranteur. Each episode he spends a week in some restaurant that's losing money and on the verge of bankruptcy. He diagnoses why the restaurant is failing and makes drastic changes in an attempt to turn it around.

As a hobby-chef and from watching these programs I've learned that that vision, ambition and even effort fail unless they are built on a foundation of basic competence in the kitchen. Sometimes, in the chef versus chef competitions, one competitor will present the judges with a creative and beautiful meal only to have them point out that the rice was mushy or the meat undercooked. In the restaurant reality shows I'm forever amazed that a business that gets so many things right can fail because the food is inconsistent or slow. The restaurant business depends on the culinary arts, and the culinary arts depend, like so many other arts, on mastering fundamentals skills. In one episode the host exposed one pretentious wannabe chef by asking him to cook an omelet, the first thing someone learns in cooking school. He burned it. You've got to walk before you can run.

It's the same in every field. You can't be a world-class musician until you master the basic notes and chords. You won't be a basketball star if you can't make a lay-up. You can't be a great author or illustrator if you don't understand basic grammar or can't draw a circle by hand.

Competence matters. You will never succeed at anything if you aren't competent in the basic skills for that position. There may be a grace period with a new job or client: your enthusiasm, humility and a willingness to learn might buy you enough time to boost your skills. But it's only buying you time. Incompetence is a time bomb: eventually someone is going to ask you to cook an omelet, and you're going to be exposed as a fraud.

This section of the book is called, "How to Make Yourself

Marketable." If you want to be in demand within your field there are two approaches that you can take. You can exaggerate your abilities and accomplishments and talk your way into jobs by making people think that you are something that you're not. You might get away with it, but I doubt it. Call it justice, or karma, the truth always floats: in the end your lies will unravel. You will fail. The alternative is to live by the truth. That means being essentially competent at your job. It doesn't guarantee success by any means. It does mean that you never have to worry about your self-promotion getting exposed as exaggeration. You can deliver on the minimum job requirements, and when the pressure is on you can execute your responsibilities. That has integrity, and over time the people around you notice that you are for real.

Let's be clear about one thing: you can't be in demand if you're incompetent. Period, end of story: there is zero demand for incompetent people. Again, you might talk your way into a job, or a series of jobs. You might fool people, for a while, with personality and pizzaz. You might be able to delegate and outsource your responsibilities for a while, but you can't hide forever.

What does it mean to be "competent" for a given job? The concept is easy to imagine, but hard to put your finger on. I gave the example of a chef cooking an omelet because that's an easy one. In reality most jobs are a complex integration of many little skills. A chef may be able to bake a cake, but if he's bad at managing the kitchen staff or keeping track of his inventory he might fail as a head chef, because in that position you not only must be a competent cook, but a competent manager of people and resources.

Some jobs are more tangible, involving focused and measurable skills, and so it's easier to evaluate competence in them. That doesn't imply anything about their importance or earning potential: digging ditches or welding pipes are focused jobs with easily measured competencies, but so are brain surgery or flying fighter jets. For lack of a better word I'm going to call these "hard skill" jobs. Training and testing people for competence in hard skill positions is a fairly straightforward thing.

On the other hand, some jobs involve mostly "soft skills" that are hard to define and measure. What does it mean for a teacher, a manager, a marketer (or a writer) to be competent? If we think about it many of the skills involved in these jobs seem to compete with each other: is it more important for a teacher to understand the subject matter or be a good communicator, even if she's communicating incorrect information? Is a good manager one who pleases his bosses, or one who wins the loyalty and brings out the best efforts of the people under her?

Soft skill jobs usually require competence at a basic cluster of tasks. The higher you climb in the ranks of your profession the more responsibilities you will need to master. Entry-level nursing, teaching or sales require basic competencies, but being a nursing supervisor, a principal or a sales manager adds to those base skills a new set of required competencies: the ability to manage people, to organize projects, to work with budgets, etc. The "Peter Principle" is a famous axiom that says that people usually get promoted beyond their competence. An effective nurse, teacher or sales representative might be put into a management position and, lacking the skills to succeed at that level, fail.

Each of us has to analyze our work, and ask ourselves what we're good at and what we're not. That can be painful, but we ought to realize that the people around us are making those determinations about us. They know what we do well, what we do poorly, and in what ways we're merely average. We need to improve in our areas of weakness or find a new job. That will happen anyway, whether we like it or not.

In the end, don't only results count? If you meet or exceed the expectations of the people who pay you, isn't that enough? That depends on how you're achieving those results. If you're getting things done because you're good at your job, even though some of your methods might be unconventional, that indicates that you're competent and can be trusted with those responsibilities again. If you only succeeded because you got lucky, or played office politics, or passed off the work of others as your own, then your incompetence will eventually catch up with you.

So far, we haven't talked about school in this book. A discussion of competence seems like the best place to bring up the subject of education. How much value does education have for career development, anyway?

A lot of my friends look at recent graduates who (in their opinion) appear completely incompetent in the workplace. I hear corporate managers grumble that recent graduates appear to be unable to function professionally in the workplace.

I believe that schools, especially colleges, should produce graduates who have core competencies, even if they lack experience. The reality is that many college graduates aren't even minimally competent when they arrive in the workplace. What conclusion should we draw from that? Should we conclude that college itself is a worthless endeavor? Should we recognize that too many colleges have become incompetent institutions themselves, unable to carry out their primary mission? Should we give up on our universities as pointless, or insist that they do a better job of graduating people that can function in the workplace?

College is essential for certain hard skill jobs. Do you want to be operated on by a surgeon who didn't go to medical school or drive over a bridge designed by someone who never went to engineering school? Do you want someone without an accounting degree to do your taxes?

What about those soft skill jobs? How many of us have thought that we could do a better job than one of our kids' teachers, even without an education degree? How many of us have been frustrated by a boss who may have had a business degree but didn't seem to have good business instincts?

Education is supposed to address this. Take the "Three R's" (reading, writing and arithmetic) for example. We assume that when someone has graduated from high school, and even more so from college, that they can read a complex document and understand it, that they can communicate in written form in a business setting and that they can do basic math. The degree is supposed to certify their basic competence in those core skills.

Can every graduate do those things? No. Can some people who didn't go to school do those things? Of course.

We need an education system that turns out competent graduates. By turning out incompetent graduates, colleges are losing credibility, but not their mission. Unfortunately, companies can no longer assume that a college degree guarantees basic competence. Graduates have to prove themselves.

So what should you do?

First, care about your profession! Life is too short to not to find satisfaction in the basic tasks that you perform everyday. What does that mean? It means that if you are a chef you find some measure of joy (yes, I used the word "joy") when you plate a well-cooked meal. It means that if you are an accountant (which I used to be) you find joy in presenting a balanced set of books. If you sell clothes, it should bring you joy to see somebody walk out the door with a suit that fits them properly. As an author, I find joy in reading over a well-crafted paragraph that I wrote, regardless of whether the book sells. If you can't enjoy your work you'll always be avoiding it, trying to delegate it to others or hopping from job to job. You will never become competent because you will never invest yourself in developing skills that feel like chores to you. If you can't enjoy the nature of your work, find new work.

Second, develop your skills. Be humble enough to know that you can always learn and improve, and always be learning and improving. Watch and listen to other people in your field: you never know when you might pick up a good idea or a new approach. Get regular training, not only to learn new things but to keep your skills sharp. Practice and develop your craft. Some jobs require this: accountants have to get periodic training in new tax laws and pilots are regularly tested and have to qualify on new equipment and procedures.

Finally, be proud of your skills. It's an old word, but approach what you do as a craftsman. Whether it's landscaping, software engineering or driving a truck, strive to master your trade. Like silversmiths or a master builders from a bygone era, we can and should approach our work as professionals, as our vocation. If we strive to "know our stuff" and be the best at what we do, we'll never be embarrassed by being unable to perform under pressure.

Let me repeat what I said earlier: there is absolutely zero demand for incompetent people. If you want to be in demand in your line of work, start by being competent. You may need more than that to succeed, but you'll never need less.

Chapter 6:
Produce

We've all heard the old clichés about how much we learn from playing sports as children: teamwork, attitude, effort, etc. Those things are mostly true, which is how they became clichés.

We should learn another lesson from youth sports. It's not as inspiring, but just as important in preparing us for life. It has to do with who starts, how much playing time everyone gets and who gets cut from the team. When we begin playing organized sports, maybe in first or second grade, everyone gets in the game and all the kids get roughly equal playing time. The goal is to have fun, teach us to know and love the game and build everyone's self-esteem. That's the way it should be: for second graders, Saturday morning soccer games aren't really about winning, they are about participating. As we get older the focus gradually shifts. By the time we get to high school sports, win-loss records start to matter. The players, the other students, the parents and administration all want to win. If the school is playing its cross-town rival, or for the state championship, the school's pride and reputation are on the line. It only becomes more so in college, and in professional sports winning is the only thing that matters (of course).

As the stakes increase, slots on the team roster, playing time and starting positions go to the players that are most likely to help the team win. The team wins by scoring points. When the risk to the team is low everyone plays, but as the cost of losing (and the reward for winning) goes up the team puts the highest scoring players in the game. If you don't produce points, you don't get minutes and you may even get cut.

This is the unpleasant lesson we need to take away from youth sports. In good times, or in organizations with nothing at stake, performance takes a back seat to participation. Companies and customers will tolerate employees that don't produce much. When jobs or profits get tight, or when the potential rewards get big, the players that score the most play the most. The others get cut.

Let me make this clear: if you want to be in demand as an employee or contractor, produce results. Of course quality matters, but when organizations keep score, quantity will beat quality almost every time.

As a recruiter I've seen this a thousand times. A company is running a search to fill a position, and I send over several candidates. Yes, the intangibles do count, but most of the time the job is going to go to the candidate with the resume that has produced the most in their previous positions. Winners get results: grades, sales, profits, championships, whatever. Students with low GPA's don't get accepted to the top schools. Salespeople that don't meet or exceed their quotas, or managers that don't create profits, or football coaches with losing seasons all find themselves looking for new jobs.

When the economy is tough, and businesses realize that their survival is at stake, top performers are in demand and everyone else's position is at risk.

Some jobs have rather obvious scoreboards: sales, profits, stock prices, how many widgets got made per shift, things like that. With other jobs it's less clear how results should be measured: teacher, accountant, graphic designer. Sometimes, in these professions, only failure gets noticed enough to make one stand out from the pack.

It would be unrealistic to deny that other factors do come into play. Favoritism, politics, likability, etc., are all reasons why marginal producers get and keep jobs. That's a lot like the youth sports we talked about earlier: when the stakes are low, scoring points doesn't matter as much. When the stakes go up, when the company is losing money and the organization is threatened, "What have you done for me lately?" becomes, "What have you done for me this month?" or even, "What are you doing for me right now?"

Let's talk about something so obvious we shouldn't have to bring it up, but I'm continually amazed by how many people I've interviewed don't grasp it. That's your worth to the organization. Start by taking what you've recently produced for the company, however it's measured, and subtract from it what you cost, in salary, expenses, etc. Now factor in your intangibles: how much your coworkers like you, the quality of what you do, how many complaints the boss gets from customers about you. Now we're figuring out what you are really worth to your employer. You may be a high producer (that helps you), but very expensive (that hurts you) and everyone loves to work with you (that saves you). You can see all the possible combinations: one employee gets low results, costs a lot but is beloved by everyone, so people make excuses for him as long as possible; another one produces a lot, but isn't worth the cost and trouble she creates, and so she's gone when the stakes go up.

Some people have a talent for blending into the background and not getting noticed. They find their way onto teams where their work gets pooled with that of others, they take positions with less visibility or fuzzier metrics, they burrow themselves into a protected niche or move around a lot before anyone notices that they never accomplish a lot. That strategy can work until hard times come to the organization, or until there's a change of management. Then there's no place to hide.

Turnover in management can move the performance goalposts. A manager might hire you to fill a particular spot on his team, or to focus on some objective in her management plan. What happens if that manager leaves for another organization, or retires, or is downsized? What happens if there is a change in the upper management structure, or the CEO announces a new strategy? You might find that "there's a new sheriff in town," and your performance is going to be measured against new standards. Your old boss might have considered you a valuable producer, but you might find yourself suddenly redundant or obsolete.

In other chapters I talk about your costs and likability, but for this discussion let's focus on production. As we've just seen, production isn't the only factor in the equation when companies decide who's on their team and who gets to play the most, but it's surely one of the best ways to tip the scales in your favor. If you are a high producer you still might get cut, but the company has to really think about it before letting you go. If the company has a lot at stake (intense competition, struggling to remain profitable) a high producer has to be really expensive or a really big jerk to get cut. While it may irk the rest of us to the depth of our beings, the superstar performers in most organizations can get away with just about anything. They become like rock stars.

Life just keeps imitating high school, huh? Win the state championship and you can write your own ticket. Drop the ball in clutch situations and you get cut from the team.

I recognize that this whole topic makes some of you sick to your stomach. You're just not wired as a results oriented person. You prefer people, process and principles. You hated it when everyone chose up sides for basketball in gym class, because you knew that you'd get chosen last. You understood, painfully well, that you never scored any points. When the game was volleyball you stood there, silently wishing for the ball to NOT come toward you so that you wouldn't be embarrassed when it hit you in the forehead. You know that companies measure results, and maybe your career ambition is or was to find a job that isn't so results oriented.

To you I say: thank goodness for your spirit. The world

needs all of us, with all of our personality types. I've spent my career recruiting hard-charging, get-it-done type people and they can be exhausting. I'm grateful for those who care about quality, integrity and the feelings of others more than sales and profits.

I'd like to challenge you, as well. I don't think that people and production are necessarily at odds with each other. We don't expect kindergarten teachers to be "results oriented," but that's because we typically think of results as sales, profits and awards. Yet a teacher who genuinely cared about her students would want as many as possible to score well on tests, as few as possible to fall behind and all of them to move on to the first grade. If a teacher did that, year in and year out, they would produce quite a legacy.

I once saw a movie that powerfully demonstrated how productivity can be overlooked, even by the producer. *Mr. Holland's Opus* came out in 1995, and it starred Richard Dreyfus, playing a music teacher named Glenn Holland. As a young man he dreamed of being a composer and producing a great piece of music which would make him famous. Needing money to pay the rent while he pursued his life's work he took a job as a high school music teacher. Over the next thirty years he was so busy with life that he never got around to finishing his composition. After three decades budget cuts force the school to eliminate the music program, and Mr. Holland loses his job. He is, of course, tempted to be bitter and regret wasting his life without producing his great work. On his last day a few students lead him to the school auditorium for what is supposed to be a retirement party. When he walks in he finds hundreds of his former students filling the room, all testifying to the profound influence his teaching had on their lives, including the state governor. They have found the sheet music for the composition he has been working on all his life, and they take up instruments, allowing him to conduct them in its first performance.

The film touched me, and many of those who've seen it, because it helps us to see that what we produce isn't always understood and recognized, even by us.

Of course the film is also a sobering reminder of my point in this chapter: in the end, Mr. Holland sees that while his life's work has had meaning and results beyond what the world measures, the music program is still eliminated by budget cuts. Even the governor, tearfully praising Mr. Holland in the final scene, can't save his job. The business world keeps score. One of the best ways to be in demand, to stay on the team and in the game, is to put points on the board.

Chapter 7:
Follow the Money

One of the constant complaints about government leaders is that they don't understand the business world. People who have spent years in the school of hard knocks, learning how to generate revenue, make payroll and turn a profit resent that politicians and bureaucrats don't seem to comprehend what it takes to run a business. The government never has to win customers, because it has no competitors and it can compel revenue through taxes. This is especially irritating to business people when these government leaders try to regulate or pontificate on how private enterprise operates.

Politicians, of course, often understand how the cash flow works for them. That's one of the things that frustrates ordinary citizens: politicians and bureaucrats have an uncanny ability to know where the money is and how to position themselves to benefit from that knowledge.

I've spent many years volunteering and working with non-profit organizations, and have nothing but respect for the way they have to compete for funds. Still, business people get frustrated sometimes with those who work in the nonprofit world for not understanding the pressures and demands of the marketplace. Like those who go into government, many of those who choose nonprofit careers don't spend too much time thinking about money and balance sheets.

Even though we may not like to think about it, governments and non-profits run on the lifeblood of cash. If the money stops flowing staff doesn't get paid, materials don't get bought, buildings aren't paid for, etc. Anyone inside government or a nonprofit who says that money doesn't matter hasn't watched what happens when budgets get cut, or there is a spending freeze. Even those who don't normally pay attention to the money become very aware of it when it's running out.

If this focus on cash sounds unsavory, it's not. If you care about curing some disease, feeding hungry people, giving refugees medical care and clean water or rescuing abused pets then you need to care about the money, because none of that can happen without resources. Anyone can talk about helping the needy or disaster relief, but action has a price tag.

In the years I've spent working with non-profits, particularly orphanages in Haiti and Europe, I've noticed that the best leaders in these places understand where the resources are, how they come in and how to use them for maximum effect. They aren't motivated by making money for themselves but they become effective at using money as a tool to help the poorest children in the world to have a chance at a better life. Leaders who understand money are in demand, even in government and non-profits.

Let me offer two pieces of advice, if you want to stay in demand: first, "get" the cash flow; second, "get into" the cash flow.

When I say "get" the cash flow I mean you must understand how and why your business or organization actually makes money. It may seem obvious: customers buy your products or clients pay invoices. Sometimes it's more complicated than that because some businesses make most of their money from a less obvious revenue stream.

Let's consider some fun examples: movie theaters, theme parks and sports franchises. The obvious source of revenue is ticket sales, and so it would seem that the obvious way to make them more successful would be to make the movies or the rides better or to win more games. In most instances the ticket sales barely cover, or don't completely cover, the operating costs of those types of operations. All of them make most of their profit from additional revenue streams like concessions sales. Putting a better sound system in the theater might satisfy the audience, but if it keeps them from getting up to buy popcorn it might hurt profits. If longer movies or rides results in fewer customers per day (three showing per theater per evening versus four, or people spending more time on the rides and less time walking past the cotton candy carts) they might hurt the bottom line.

To be an in-demand-employee you have to be smart about the money. As I said in another chapter, one of my favorite shows involves a famous chef/restauranteur who visits failing restaurants and tries to figure out how to turn them around.

The episodes of this show have a common theme: there are lots of ways to lose money in the restaurant business. In one episode the owner wouldn't lower his prices, clinging to the idea that he was getting more per meal even thought the high prices were driving customers away. In another episode, a chef was buying too many prepared ingredients (like pre-sliced vegetables), believing that it was saving time in the kitchen. He had to learn that properly trained prep chefs could save money by doing these tasks themselves. In another episode there were too many choices on the menu, forcing the restaurant to move slowly and have high inventory costs. In another, the place was full, but all the customers had two-for-one coupons the restaurant was running in the local paper, and finally, in another episode the elaborate menus meant the tables weren't turning fast enough.

I love that show because many of the lessons are transferable to any business. What we learn is that there are many different ways to make or lose money in a business, and that some people "get" that and some don't.

Some people are just savvy and clever about how money works, and some aren't. That is partly a function, no doubt, of their personality type (more about that in a moment) and some is a function of experience. For example, where did you learn your first lessons about money? Did your parents run a small business? Did you hear about the family shop or farm around the dinner table, and go to work for it as a kid? That's no guarantee that you learned anything, but it certainly gave you an early advantage in grasping basic business principles. The kind of things you learn in small business "scale up" (to use business jargon) to bigger companies. You learn early how to understand the differences between revenue and profit, how to figure your costs and manage cash flow.

Some employees never grasp the difference between profit centers and cost centers within a company. They can't fathom how, although they are valuable or even essential, they are still an overhead cost to the company rather than a revenue or profit generator. Some employees resent that sales people usually keep their jobs when times get tough and are the first ones hired back. The reason for this, of course, is that the company needs to keep cash flowing, and sales people do that. If they don't, the company will get new sales people. Without someone bringing revenue in the door, all the other bright and experienced employees that make or create or manage the product will be out of work.

Let me put it this way: not everyone who "gets" the cash flow (understands the financial dynamics of the company) is in demand, but everyone who is in demand "gets" the cash flow. Valuable players always seem to "get it," they instinctively understand how the organization works, how it makes money and where the profit and cost centers are.

My second piece of advice, if you want to be in demand: then "get in" the cash flow. What I mean is that the most secure positions in any company are those that positively affect the businesses bottom line. If you want to be the first hired and the last to be let go, be someone that directly makes money for your employer. In the last chapter, on producing, we talked about scoring points for your company. Industry awards and accolades are great, but there are no points more valuable than dollars. To put it bluntly: make money for the organization and you will be in demand. Bring money with you and the organization will want you and offer whatever it takes to get you.

So how do you do that? How do you get into the cash flow? Obviously, it depends on your profession: how does a snow plow driver or a nurse or an airline pilot get into the cash flow? Without writing a longer book on basic business principles, let me here just offer some "do's" and "don'ts" for those seeking an in-demand-career.

- *Do: pay attention to the company's business model.* Do you understand how the company gets paid? Particularly, do you understand the revenue, profit and cost centers?

- *Don't: assume, EVER, that this isn't your problem.* You may think that people higher up in the organization know what they're doing, but that's not always true. If it doesn't make sense, it might not be sensible. In the last few years we've seen some of America's biggest and most powerful corporations being run into the ground because people at the top didn't grasp how to make money. Some understood how to generate their own bonuses while wrecking the business.

- **Do: contribute to generate revenue in your area.** Put "points on the board" for your company, even if you're not in a direct cash role. If you're an airline pilot or gate agent you can win or lose customers by how you interact with them. Understand that everyone in an organization is involved in selling and trying to increase profits, and everyone can chase customers into the arms of a competitor.

- **Don't: become a transparent mercenary.** Naked ambition, pushiness or disregard for your co-workers is ugly. Everyone is working for themselves, but there is a way to do that with grace and dignity. Those who live by the sword in their careers will die by the sword when the company's politics shift.

- **Do: find ways to increase profitability in your area**. Everyone can find ways to increase profits. Clever employees understand that it doesn't matter how much money is flowing through the company if it's flowing out faster than it comes in. Workers who find ways to capture more profit will always be in demand, and everyone can do that in their area.

- **Don't: cost the company too much by screwing up constantly.** Bad decisions or irresponsible behavior will catch up with you, eventually. In good times, when the company is fat with cash, waste might be overlooked. When things tighten up those who have a reputation for waste and poor management will be the first to go.

- **Do: choose jobs that are in profit centers.** Not everyone can do this, of course. If you're worried about being in demand, especially in a tight economy, and you have a choice between making the company money or being overhead you should consider the position that puts you in the cash flow, rather than outside of it.

- **Don't: try to be something you're not or do something that you're not good at.** If you don't belong in sales don't be a sales representative. All of us can grow, and sometimes we are forced to, but you do no one, especially yourself or your family, any favors by being a square peg in a round hole.

To wrap this chapter up let's shift from how the company makes money to how you make money, in salary, bonuses, etc.

As a recruiter I deal with negotiating compensation packages every day, and I find that there's quite a bit of confusion about how these packages get computed. It really is quite simple. People aren't paid more because they're smarter, nicer, better educated, more qualified, or even more involved in the core business. Pay is usually based on how much revenue and profit that employee is expected to contribute to the organization. I often hear people complaining about how some sales representative makes more than an engineer. After all, doesn't the engineer design the product and understand the technology?

That may be true, but the salesperson brings cash into the company, and the compensation package reflects that difference. I could give similar examples, but hopefully you get the idea.

If you want to be in demand, and have that reflected in job offers, job security or compensation, then "get" how the business makes money and "get into" the revenue stream by contributing to the bottom line.

Chapter 8:
Manners Maketh the Man

In 1964 the Academy Award for Best Picture went to *My Fair Lady,* along with seven other Oscars. It's the story of Henry Higgins, a professor of Phonetics (the study of pronunciation) and a poor young woman named Eliza Doolittle who sells flowers in the streets of London. Professor Higgins is an arrogant English aristocrat who believes that people's accent, their pronunciation and tones when speaking, determine their prospects in society. In other words, Higgins believes that the poor are doomed to poverty because they cannot speak well enough to advance to the upper classes. He wagers another friend of his that by using his techniques he can teach any woman from the streets to speak well enough to be passed off as a duchess at the upcoming Embassy Ball. Eliza is chosen as the test subject, and in the scene quoted above Higgins is trying to break her Cockney (working-class London) accent which drops the "H" sound at the beginning of words. By the end of the film Higgins has transformed Eliza from a Cockney street vendor into a woman who moves at ease within aristocratic society.

The movie was based on a 1912 stage play, *Pygmalion,* by

George Bernard Shaw that dealt with issues that troubled late nineteenth century Britain. The Industrial Revolution and urbanization had created a huge underclass. The cities were full of terrible slums, and the factories used armies of child laborers. The mean streets of London that Charles Dickens wrote about in his novels were quite real, and many people in England began to think and write about the urban poor and the probable fate of the "street urchins" that they saw everywhere. At the same time, Charles Darwin wrote a book that changed the world, *The Origin of Species,* introducing the idea of Evolution.

These influences combined to develop an idea called *social darwinism,* or *social determinism.* The notion was that people were doomed to be merely products of their environment and class. According to this line of reasoning, poverty, underemployment or unemployment produced certain types of people: cunning (in the ways of survival) but not clever; mean-spirited not generous; violent not refined. Unemployment (or underemployment) made one crude, bitter, unable to speak well, wary of strangers or other cultures, incapable of entrepreneurship or leadership. It robbed one of the ability to appreciate art, culture or literature. Some aristocrats saw it as their burden to reach down and help the poor, bitter underclass by sharing bits of their wisdom and culture. They figured that the victims of Britain's cycles of economic change were hopeless without the work of do-gooders like them.

What's interesting about *Pygmalion* is Shaw's notion that someone's language could raise their station in life. Eliza Doolittle's life is changed because she learns to speak well, display proper manners and be gracious to others. Those things change not only her life but her fortunes.

In Demand People are from every industry, region, ethnic group, job type and educational background. Most of them have one thing in common, though: people want to have them around. Yes, there are specialists who are so good at what they do that their employers and clients will tolerate them being unlikable. As a general rule, more likable people are more in demand. There are a lot of factors that go into being likable, but the ability to speak well is essential. I'm not talking about public speaking, or the ability to give a sales pitch, but communicating to others clearly, pleasantly and in a way that encourages the people around you. Think about it: can you imagine someone being in demand as an employee or contractor who is rude, discouraging or can't explain the product or service clearly?

How well do you speak? I'm not just asking whether you use proper grammar and pronunciation (although that does matter, especially in a job search) but do you speak well: well of others, well of the world around you, well of your situation, well of yourself?

Language has tremendous power to shape our perceptions. How we describe a person, place or thing, what we name it, often controls how we understand it. In politics both sides try be the first to give names to problems or proposed solutions. Public perception of a law or government program is shaped by how it is labeled, especially in the media. Sick people often feel better once a diagnosis is made because it gives a name to their ailment.

How do you describe things in your career? What names are you giving to former employers, your career, your financial situation, your prospects, your skills, possible jobs or people around you? Just in the last week I've spoken to several people who are unemployed, have lost all or most of the equity in their homes and have seen their pensions or retirement accounts wiped out. They were planning to retire sometime in the next decade and spending the following twenty or thirty years enjoying themselves. I've been struck by the different language that they used to describe their situations. One guy sees himself as "screwed." He "has nothing." There are "no jobs for an old guy" like him. He "has to get a crummy job" because his house is "a boat anchor" around his neck. Another guy in almost identical circumstances, admits that he has "challenges" but sees "opportunities" not problems. He and his wife now have an "opportunity" to start a small business that they've always dreamed of and "twenty-five years to grow it into something." They see this as the "beginning of a new life" that reminds them of when they first got married. As for the house, they're thankful that they have one, but "it's just a house" and "home is wherever we make a life." Another guy I talked to said that he and his wife have always dreamed of becoming missionaries. They see this time as an "opportunity" to follow that dream "ahead of schedule" and are considering moving to work in a missionary school and hospital complex in the mountains of Central America.

I just Googled the phrase "positive language" and Google

listed 65,900 pages on the Web that mention those terms. In the last few years the business world, educational institutions and self-help books have been buzzing about the power of positive language to shape perceptions and behaviors. It's easy to roll one's eyes and dismiss it all as happy talk for a feel-good culture. Even the Old Testament Bible recognizes the power of positive language. The Book of Proverbs, chapter 16, verses 23-24 tells us that, "A wise man's heart guides his mouth, and his lips promote instruction. Pleasant words are a honeycomb, sweet to the soul and healing to the bones."

The point is that the wise man uses language to not only instruct but to nourish himself and those around him. The fifty-somethings above were all facing unemployment and delayed retirement. Which among them do you think provided useful instruction and healing, down into the bones, for themselves and their families?

A person who speaks positively will advance in society, just as Eliza Doolittle did in *My Fair Lady*. I guarantee that an unemployed person who speaks this way will have many more job prospects and a vastly more successful job search than the person who names and frames everything negatively.

The person who chooses to rant about their problems or speak about everything in negative or derogatory terms only makes a bad situation worse, and risks making their problems permanent features of their life. Again, the Book of Proverbs stresses this point (chapter 10, verse 10): *"A chattering fool comes to ruin. The mouth of the righteous is a fountain of life, but violence overwhelms the mouth of the wicked."*

Please note this: the measure of your character is not how you speak to people that can benefit you. If you're polite and thoughtful only to those who can pay or promote you, what does that reveal about your character? That's nothing but shrewd self-interest. People with integrity show equal respect to those who can do nothing for them. How do you treat the cleaning crew in your office, the food worker in the cafeteria or the workers in the call center? I remember a famous author and television personality who said that when he would see a business traveler being rude to a flight attendant or a waiter in restaurant he would approach and ask for their business card. The businessperson would be flattered and polite, thinking that this celebrity was somehow going to advance their career. He would thank them for the card and tell them that he would be writing a letter to tell their CEO how this employee treats people when traveling on company business. Ouch.

For some people, negative and critical language has become so ingrained they aren't even aware they speak that way. When we have a bad habit we can't demand that everyone around us accept it, we have to change. The way to change bad habits is to replace them with positive habits.

Every few weeks a bus pulls up in front of some low buildings and young men and women file out while a sergeant shouts at them to form a line. The sergeant berates them for the ineptness of their line and bemoans that this is, without a doubt, the worst group of recruits that he has ever been forced to set his eyes upon. Over the next few hours they get new haircuts, clothes and routines. They are exercised relentlessly, taught how and when to salute, who to apply the term, "Sir" to and who to never call "Sir" (i.e., the sergeant, who will yell back, "Don't call me 'Sir.' I work for a living!"). A few months later their families come to their graduation, and moms and dads don't recognize their own child when they march out onto the tarmac. They have been transformed from the kid that they knew into something else: United States Marines.

The Marine Corps knows the same thing that William of Wykeham, the English Bishop of Winchester in the fourteenth century, knew. He was famous for saying, and placing on his coat of arms, the statement: Manners Makyth Man, famously remembered as the truism that Manners Maketh the Man. It's true that who we are springs from our heart, but William of Wykeham, like the Marine Corps, knew that teaching someone standards and codes of behavior usually modifies their actual behavior.

Like your language, your manners shape your world. Being *in demand* isn't just about what you know, but who you are, how you speak and how you behave. It's closely linked to your personal conduct, your daily routine, dress, hygiene, housekeeping, communications, interactions with others and financial habits. If you live in a disorganized, lazy and inconsiderate manner, you will, almost by definition, have a life that reflects that. If you act like a slob then it's likely that you are a slob, and your life and career will be slob-like. Unless you have some skill that is so unique and so valuable that people will tolerate this type of behavior, you will not be in demand.

When the economy is roaring and employers need warm bodies to fill slots, they'll hire and keep slobs. Even rude slobs. When the economy is in rough seas, the slobs go overboard. Especially the rude ones. Networking and job searching during a recession is an uphill battle even if you make a good impression. If you make a bad impression then it can be nearly impossible to compete for a good job.

In *My Fair Lady*, Eliza Doolittle didn't just learn to stop dropping her "H's," she learned the manners of polite society. If you moved to another country you would be wise to learn the customs and manners of that society, especially if you want to advance within it. In the same way, when you are unemployed with limited options your manners cannot only shape your life, they can open doors and make you in demand.

Chapter 9:
It

At some point we've all daydreamed about starting our own business. We imagine how great it would be to be our own boss, set our own schedule and to not be treated like an employee because we wouldn't be anyone's employee.

I've been self-employed for twenty years, and through that I've experienced some of the greatest and worst moments of my life. I've had moments of deep satisfaction and crushing despair, times when I felt tremendously self-confident and other times when I was frightened and doubted my own judgment. I've made and lost piles of money, living the high life one year and being flat broke another. In this chapter I'm going to share what I've learned about being in demand as a self-employed business owner. At first glance that might seem like a contradiction: if you're self-employed who are you in demand with? The answer, of course, is customers, clients and partners. The principles of this book apply to any business, whether you own it or not. There are a million business books out there, and while I don't know everything, there are some lessons that I've learned about surviving and thriving when you are the boss.

Here's a big one: on your first day of working for yourself you get some good news, and some bad news. The good news is that you are the boss. Yeah! The bad news is that you're the boss. Uh-oh. Let that sink in for a moment.

That means that you, and you alone, are responsible for this business. When you work for someone else you have opinions about everything, but when faced with dilemmas that have no easy solution you can always hope that someone "upstairs" has a plan to get you out the mess. When you own the company you're the one upstairs. There are no older, wiser heads to figure things out, to come to the rescue or to take the blame with creditors or customers if things go badly. No rescue helicopters are going to swoop in and pull you out of the water if you hit the rocks. You're it: if you hire employees they're looking at you to save their jobs, their health insurance, and to clean up their messes.

That's a lot of pressure. From what I've seen, some people have a certain combination of personal traits that make them able to not only withstand that pressure, but to succeed under it as well. Some people crumble, but it brings out the best in others, and they become successful and fulfilled. It's not about intelligence, wisdom, discipline or talent. Some people have all those things but thrive best inside of an organization, as a part of a team. Others may not be as smart, gifted or hardworking, but they have a certain knack for being an entrepreneur. We're tempted to say that only the brightest and most determined can succeed at running their own business, but I'm not sure that's true. As a corporate recruiter I've placed some of the most brilliant, dedicated and hardworking people inside organizations and on teams where they made huge contributions and huge incomes. I've also seen people with less intellectual ability, who work less hours, make a fortune running their own business. It's as much about temperament as talent, about personality as perseverance.

The bottom line: to "make it" as a business owner you have to have "it." I don't know how to define "it," exactly, but I know it when I see it and it's clear when someone doesn't have "it."

Because "it" is an undefinable just-right mixture of qualities, someone can have a few things going for them and still not hit the right combination for success. Consider four friends of mine who have gone into business for themselves and ask yourself if any of them have the "it" to be a successful entrepreneur.

The first is a contractor who does home remodeling projects, mostly kitchens, basement build-outs and room additions. He went into business for himself because he generally doesn't like authority figures telling him what to do. It's not that he's antisocial or radical, he just prefers to live a fairly unstructured life. He wanted free time to travel and pursue his hobbies and loved the idea of finishing a project, collecting a good-sized check and then taking some time off before the next project. The quality of his work is quite good and he's a likable guy with good networking skills. His lifestyle vision causes him to not follow through on opportunities and even satisfied clients are hesitant to recommend him because of his inconsistency. He goes through one boom and bust cycle after another, and when I see him I never know if he's going to be leaving for Europe or about to go broke.

The second friend owns a local restaurant. He opened it because he loves interesting food and is a great cook. He dreamed of turning his hobby into a business and making a living out of his passion. He is willing to work long hours, never takes a day off and doesn't really complain about it. On the other hand he's learned that when you own a business you have to pay attention to all parts of it, not just the parts that interest you. He loves dealing with the food: experimenting with the menu, dealing with his cooks, hosting tasting parties and hearing customers rave about their meals. He hates dealing with the money part of it, and so he avoids the bookkeeping and the dozens of little financial decisions a restaurant owner has to make every week. His employees can't get him to engage with business matters until things become emergencies, and then he tends to agree to anything to end the conversation quickly. As a result the restaurant bumps along, barely breaking even, and he's carrying too much debt.

The third friend owns a taxi business in a developing country I recently visited. He's not technically a friend, but I got to know him a bit when my friends and I hired him at the airport to drive us around to all our meetings for a week. We came out, stood in the cab line and he picked us up in a mini-van. On the way to our hotel he asked how long we would be in the country and when we told him he offered us a deal: instead of hiring a different cab every day, we could pay him a discounted flat rate for the week and he'd show up every morning, drive us anywhere in the city we needed to go, and bring us back to the hotel each evening. We did some quick calculations, figured that he was offering us a good deal in price and convenience, and took his offer. Over the week we got to know him a bit. He'd had a job in a factory but hated being just a worker. He wanted more control over his own life and destiny. He borrowed money from family and bought a cab. After a while he was able to upgrade to a van. A few years later he was negotiating package deals for the week like we'd agreed to, for which he took a slightly lower rate but guaranteed that his primary asset (the van) was generating revenue all day instead of having dead time between fares or sitting in a cab line. He had saved up enough to buy a second van and hired a relative to drive that, and while we were in our meeting he waited outside, directing that employee over his cell phone. He was saving up enough to buy a third van, and was steadily building his own taxi company.

The fourth friend is a software developer who had worked for a large manufacturing company for years. He and two of his friends had developed a piece of software that helped small manufacturers manage their materials inventory. They quit their jobs and started their own company to sell their application. All of them were super-bright and understood the technology and the manufacturing business extremely well. They were mature, self-controlled people with good educations who had been successful middle-management types for years. They were willing to take risks and work long hours to build a business that could make them lots of money if it would take off. The problem was that none of them had actual experience with financing a business launch. They borrowed money and sought venture capital investment. In the process they gave several other investors stock in the company so that there were six owners. Every dollar of profit had to be divided six ways, and it made it difficult for any of the partners to make enough to earn a living. They had burned through savings, and several reverted to taking day jobs which limited their ability to get out and market and sell the product.

So, which of my four friends had "it?" All of them? None of them? It's hard to say, and in the end perhaps "it" is only revealed by how things turn out. We all have strengths and weaknesses, qualities that help us in our business or limit our success. Every self-employed person will face adversity. When the going gets tough those who have "it" find a way to leverage their strengths and contain their weaknesses. Much of "it" comes from a certain temperament, perspective on life and emotional and physical health.

Sometimes, people who have "it" are *"interpreneurs."* They bring the same set of skills but work within a larger organization. Being an entrepreneur inside a bigger entity is too big a topic to discuss here, but just let me say that it is a difficult position. *Intrepreneurs* are hybrids that test everyone's tolerance and patience. Some of the people around them think they aren't loyal enough to the company and others think they're too loyal.

Intrepreneurs are always walking a fine line between being a business and being a part of their business. Even when they are successful by making money for the corporation they can make enemies by competing with or embarrassing other parts of the company. Higher ups often consider them to be loose cannons or insubordinate. They are often tolerated, but company politics can turn against them quickly. If you think that you have "it" and are functioning as an *intrepreneur* you may want to consider taking your chances and leaving the nest to really start your own business.

Entrepreneurs who have "it" are always in demand. They are never short of customers and clients who want what they're selling because they have an instinct for their market, for offering the right thing at the right price. They sense shifts in the marketplace or industry and don't get outmaneuvered by competitors. Banks will lend them money, investors buy into their ideas and other businesses want to partner with them. They recruit the right employees when and where and how they need them, and they know how to retain or let them go, if necessary.

Do you have "it"? If you don't then being self-employed will be a stressful existence that brings you little joy or success. If you do then you'll never really be fulfilled until you own your own business. Pressure and hard times will bring out the best in you, and you'll feel energized every morning that you wake up and live by your wits and efforts.

Section III:
"Sell Yourself"

Chapter 10:
Tell Your Story

Being qualified is not enough.

Many people go through life thinking that it is. They're convinced that because they have the right degree or certificate or required experience, they have what it takes to get a job. Qualifications will only get you considered, they don't get you chosen unless there is no one else who's qualified.

Do you choose friends because they're "qualified" to be your friend? To work with or collaborate with someone on a project? (Think of all-star teams, where everyone is qualified, but there is no chemistry or synergy between the players.). Do you fall in love with someone because they're "qualified?" Do you choose products or services or restaurants because they're "good enough?"

Skills are a minimum requirement for a position, but not enough to compete against other people with the same skills. Just about everyone who applies for highly desirable jobs is qualified. What sets you apart? It isn't just that you are more qualified. You can't just win it on some point scale. It takes something more to be in demand in the marketplace. You have to market yourself, especially in a competitive job market. It's rarely just a contest of qualifications. You have to connect with your customer, which in the job market is the person who makes the hiring decisions.

Your goal should be to let someone know who you are, beyond just what you've done. Once you're in the door somewhere, no one cares about your resume anymore. It's what kind of person you are, and what you can bring to the organization, that matters. Most people who are doing the hiring realize this. They're looking for someone that they want to have around.

Here's a hard truth about the world: people get hired by other people, and stories matter to people.

Let's be clear: people lie about this all the time. They like to say that they're objective and only care about qualifications and measurable factors. That makes them sound smart and fair, and everyone likes to think that they're smart and fair. What's interesting is that when they start talking about someone that they know, work with, hired or are considering hiring, they ask for more information. Something like, "Hey, Sally, how did the interviews go? Anybody interesting?" If you ask them about coworkers or interviewees they tell you something interesting about them, both positively and negatively: this guy is a son of immigrants who grew up in the inner city, or this one is an ex-jock whose still living in the glory days and thinks that he's God's gift to women!

Political campaigns always frame their candidate in terms of their story: McCain was an admiral's son and a POW for five years; Obama is the black son of an immigrant, raised by a single mother, who went to Harvard; Bush was a president's son and spoiled frat guy who quit drinking when he was forty; Palin is a hockey mom; JFK was a rich kid and war hero with a glamorous wife; Lincoln was born in a log cabin and never told a lie. You get the idea.

Sports writers and promoters know this in their gut. Their business is only minimally about staging a competition. Fan and endorsements come from the drama of the story surrounding an athlete. That's what makes the competition interesting. Fans have to connect with him or her to cheer them on. In any sport, we as spectators need more than the action: we need a bigger narrative. We see it in everything from football to golf. The Olympics are always marketed on those narratives: think about all those "up close and personal" video packages during the Olympic coverage.

No one likes to admit that they are affected by the bigger narrative, but they are all convinced that everyone else is. They say things like, "I don't fall for all that fluff. I'm voting for Candidate X because of the objective policy issues," or, "I don't care about any of the drama around that quarterback, I just appreciate his stats." For example, Lance Armstrong is a superstar because even people who don't care about bike racing care that he beat cancer to win the Tour de France seven times. Lance understands this, which is why his autobiography was called It's Not About the Bike.

Qualifications merely get you into the game, they don't win it for you. Both teams at the Superbowl, or everyone in the U.S. Open golf tournament, is good at what they do and deserves to be there. Winning takes something more. To have people want you to win, to cheer for you, it takes a compelling narrative, a story that connects with the fans.

Don't misunderstand me: I'm not talking about manipulating the truth. That always backfires because integrity matters, and you can't pull the lie off for long. The fake story always gets exposed.

Any good personal story has certain elements:

- **Point of View (POV)**. From what perspective is the story told? The same person can be a hero or villain, depending on the perspective of the narrative. For example, Candidate X might be portrayed as "a man of the people, fighting for the little guy by standing up to the fat cats," or "an angry rabble-rouser tearing down our traditions." A prospective employee might be considered "a prima donna bailing out on her existing employer when the company hits a hard patch and her perks get cut", or "a star performer seeking new challenges."

- **Relevance.** Who cares? What's "the hook?" What's interesting about you? If you were dating someone, and they were telling their parents about you, what would they focus on? They wouldn't say that you're "qualified," as in, "he'll do." Imagine that you have a friend who works somewhere you would like to get hired, and you learn there is an open position. They've received resumes from more than a hundred people who are just as qualified as you. Your friend happens to find herself in line at the coffee bar next to the president of the company. She gets just a couple of minutes before their orders are up to "hook" his interest in you. What would you want her to say? What about you is interesting in a way that's relevant to the company? Is there anything distinctive or unique about you that adds extra value to the company?

• **Plot.** What's your narrative? A plot involves some problem that's solved, something that is overcome. Think about all those athlete stories at the Olympics that the network sports writers find and develop. There's always some adversity, some impossible odds they have or must overcome. Stuff like: "an aging champion trying to win one more time;" "a former favorite trying to recover from a potentially career-ending injury;" "an outsider from the wrong side of the tracks, trying to prove they belong;" or "an eccentric long shot chasing a dream;" and on and on. If you pay attention, you'll realize that they only have about eight or ten basic plots, and only the details change. People watch, to a large degree, because they're drawn in by the human plot lines. NASCAR is more popular in the U.S. than Formula One because NASCAR markets the drivers, while Formula One markets the car technology. Americans relate to the drivers' personalities and stories, while they don't know or understand the F1 drivers. The same thing can be said for other sports: we pay attention to the World

Cup or the Tour de France if Americans with a compelling story are in it, but we don't know the European players' stories, so most of the time we don't care. Products, brands and businesses have plot lines associated with them, as do contractors and employees.

• **Compelling Structure.** A well-told story or narrative is not always framed chronologically. A classic plot line contains some problem that is exposed, a conflict or struggle to resolve that problem, and some resolution. That order isn't necessarily chronological. For example, we might tell the story of Bill Gates in one of two ways. We might say: "Bill Gates was a nerdy Seattle kid who got really into computers, then started working on the idea of the personal computer in college. He dropped out of college when he saw an opportunity to start a company that made operating systems for IBM. He built that company into Microsoft, one of the world's largest corporations and helped to create the Information Revolution." That would be accurate, but it's not the most interesting way to tell his story. We might instead say: "The Information Revolution has changed human life as we know it, and it might not have happened but for the most unlikely of revolutionaries: a nerdy kid from Seattle who dropped out of college to challenge one of the world's most powerful corporations." They're both the same story, but which has the most interesting structure? Which one intrigues you the most? Those are both one sentence stories (albeit long sentences). Narrative structure is crucial, no matter how long or short the story.

Before you can tell your story, you have to discover it. Most of us don't have that sort of perspective on ourselves. It feels conceited and dramatic. We're uncomfortable with people that promote themselves with some grandiose self-narrative.

Let's be clear: I don't want you to go out and market yourself with some silly, exaggerated tale that makes you sound like a movie hero or celebrity athlete. I do think that you should have some compelling way to tell your story that will make you stand out to potential employers or customers. As we've seen, they are going to have some story about you in mind anyway. Are you going to frame that story or will they? Will your competitors?

Discovering your story involves honest self-examination and, probably, input from others. Sometimes we can't stand back far enough from ourselves to really see what is interesting or unique about us. People that are very close to us might have the same problem. Sometimes it takes people that are close enough to know you, but not so close that they can't see the forest through the trees.

To construct your story, ask yourself the following questions.

What's interesting about you? Especially, what's humanly interesting about you. It's probably something in your story, not even in your qualifications or accomplishments. What would be intriguing or distinct? It may not even be technically relevant to your field. You might be applying for a job as an engineer, but the fact that you're a concert pianist who started out on a music scholarship might make people say, "Hmmmm." So might the fact that you were raised by missionaries in Indonesia, even if you're applying for a job as a financial analyst. The fact that you run ultra-marathons or mastered the art of French cooking might catch peoples interest, even if you're applying for medical school.

What's your plot or story arc? What narrative are you bringing to the workplace? Are you the angry young man taking on the establishment? Are you the white kid from the suburbs who's backpacked around the world and is passionate about working cross-culturally? Are you the brilliant genius and rising star seeking to make your mark on the world? Are you the disadvantaged or disabled kid who overcomes all obstacles? Are you the alpha male or female who always wins? Are you the eclectic and eccentric trailblazer? You get the idea. Here's one thing that it can't be: you're a great guy or gal who's great at everything and is great-looking, too. No one is going to buy that, and it's not interesting. Successful people's stories always frame their accomplishments in the context of some interesting narrative or in spite of some obstacle. Notice that all of those examples are one sentence arcs with a POV (point of view). When scriptwriters "pitch" a script to agents or production companies, they have to preface it with a "log line," a one-sentence hook description like the ones above. You aren't going to do that with your resume or CV, but people who read it and interview you are going to (maybe subconsciously) assign a log line to your story. Do you know what that is?

Is the POV of your story relevant to the employer? What benefit does it bring to them? How does it solve their problems? I wouldn't be too inclined to hire the angry young anarchist who wants to change the world. I might wish you luck, but please start your revolution in someone else's company or department. Nor would I be too eager to take on the aspiring diva seeking a stage on which to perform. Those might be really intriguing log lines on the CD or novel, but a hiring committee isn't going to see any value from their POV. That's not an establishment thing but a team thing: the tortured artist or wild rebel narrative is interesting (I might read his autobiography or watch his movie), but don't want to have him on my payroll or have to work on projects with him.

How do you tell that story in an interesting way? What do you lead with? How do you support it? What's the close? Are you the goal oriented team player looking for a team that's making a difference together? That's cool, but if you're going to write a few hundred words about yourself, what are some compelling elements from your life that illustrate that? How can you structure those so that I'm drawn into the story? These are the elements of good writing. If you're not a great writer, get help from someone who is.

In the end, your story should not answer all the questions about you. Otherwise there would be no reason to call you in for an interview to learn more. A story can be short, intriguing and make whoever hears it itching to hear the rest. It's said that the novelist Ernest Hemingway's friend bet him ten dollars that he couldn't write a novel with six words. He thought about it and wrote: Baby shoes. For sale. Never worn. He collected the ten bucks. Can you tell your story in a way that makes people want to meet you?

Chapter 11:
Networking

Unless we are celebrities or professional sales people, most of us try to keep our world small and manageable. We can only afford to have so many friendships, get to know so many people, and go to so many events. Most of us like to keep our world inside comfortable and familiar boundaries. When times are good, this is a great way to live. To be in demand throughout our career we need to grow our world, because a bigger world means more opportunities. In Demand People have more connections and relationships, spread far and wide through a variety of companies or organizations. They know that their success is directly proportional to their web of relationships. I'm not making the tired old point that, "It's not what you know but who you know," because it's both, with some other things thrown in as well. Even so, knowing people is the key to getting interviews, so the more people that you can know the more interviews you are likely to get. If your web of relationships grows—if you come to know more people in more companies in more places—your world effectively gets bigger, and your opportunities become more plentiful.

Mastering the art of professional networking is one of the key qualities of being and staying in demand. At one level it's relatively simple to understand, and technology has made it easier than ever. You know ten people, each of them knows ten people, and so on. Networking is connecting with people in exponentially expanding circles, so that the number of people that you "know" is vast. Social networking websites make the mechanics of these connections relatively simple. You have a list of friends, and if you click on any of their faces on your page then you can see a list of their friends. You can invite those people on their friends list to join your friends list. Everybody can see a running list of one-line updates about what everyone is doing at the moment. I just checked my Twitter feed and discovered that a "friend" that I follow in England just got back from rehearsal and was having tea and toast while another "friend" in Texas is at their daughter's parent-teacher conference. I just let the world (everyone who subscribes to my feed and the feeds of my feed) know that I was at my desk and writing about how to network.

So Facebook and other sites have made networking easy, right? Not exactly. These relationships are superficial at best. I might learn what someone in San Diego's favorite ice cream flavor is or that someone in London moved into a new apartment. That doesn't help me to get funding for my startup business, sell copies of this book or find a job. It's considered bad form to exploit these sites to sell or ask for favors. Networking should increase the quality as well as the quantity of your relationships. That being said, even large, relatively superficial networks can be a starting point from which to develop more serious professional relationships. For example, I can't exactly post, "I need a job" on Facebook and hope to get many responses, but there are professional networking sites where I can develop business contacts.

You can abuse and waste your networking opportunities. It's far too easy to alienate people in networking situations, making certain that they will never introduce you to their friends or do you favors. This afternoon, as I was writing and periodically checking my email and Facebook, I got another post from a friend of mine who exploits every opportunity to blatantly promote whatever money-making scheme he's into this month. I have other friends who launch rants about politics, complain about their jobs or detail all their physical ailments. Please listen to what I am about to tell you: there is an art to networking and advancing professional connections. That art is grounded in genuine respect for people, their time and their feelings. Most people do not want to click a link to your multilevel marketing website. Few people want to be trapped next to you at a dinner party while you pester them to get you a job. No one wants to have you go through your sales pitch every time that they run into you at church or the gym. Networking is not seeing everyone around you as a "lead." There are books and tapes and workshops that will tell you that it is, and there are people that have made quite a bit of money treating the people around them like that. Trust me: most people resent and avoid being treated as a "lead." If you adopt that approach people will start avoiding you.

One more thought about what networking is not. It is not a list of disinterested contacts that have no interest in hearing from you. For example, a number of years ago a friend of mine took a job running sales and marketing for a relatively small firm. During interviews leading up to the job, the CEO of the firm kept telling him that the firm had an extensive and high quality network of industry contacts across the country that would provide a foundation for taking the firm to the next level. On his first day he sat down in the CEO's office to begin reviewing these connections and making an action plan. What he discovered was that the firm had purchased lists of "leads" from one of the many marketing companies that provide such lists. The truth was that this was essentially direct mail or phonebook data: the marketing company had the name, business address and name of someone within hundreds of companies almost randomly spread across various states. In some cases the data was more than a year old. The CEO, who did not have good people skills and had alienated most of his actual clients over the course of his career, had taken to buying these lists and cold-calling companies to see if they would be interested in his products. My friend had expected to develop and leverage a professional network of former clients and partner firms. Instead he had to lead the marketing and sales people through what was essentially a direct mail and cold-calling plan, starting from scratch without any name recognition for the firm they were representing.

There is nothing wrong with cold-calling from lists of names or directories. Yet there is an important difference between a network of human connections or referrals and cold-calling people that you have no relationship with. Cold calling can lead to sales and jobs, for sure, and you have to engage in it, especially in a tight job market. It may be the only way to get your foot in the door and make a connection. Yet it is always better, if possible, to grow your world by building relationships.

Networking is valuable for all sorts of reasons, personally and professionally. If you have a passion for ice-fishing, totem pole carving or yodeling competitions, then you can find other people that share your passion and pass on information and tips. You can go to gatherings, subscribe to newsletters and get introduced to people all around the world like yourself. There's a real buzz in the group because you all want the same thing.

Networking for a job is fundamentally different from social networking. Not everyone in your network wants the same thing; lots of them want things that are mutually exclusive. It's what's known as a zero-sum game: if someone wins then someone else must lose. You want a job. Some employer has a job to give, but he doesn't care about giving it to you; he just wants to solve his problem, whatever it is, as quickly, efficiently and cheaply as possible. He wants to find the right person but he does not want to be pestered constantly by unqualified or unlikeable applicants. Other people that you are networking with also want that same job. They aren't going to cooperate with you: after all, you aren't just fellow fans of some rock band, sharing stories and tips about upcoming concerts. You are competitors for a job which both of you need to feed your families. The person you are talking to may not want to introduce you to their best contacts because he may be working them for himself or on behalf of another friend or relative.

Networking for a job requires diplomacy, judgment and advice. You must think of it as an obstacle course: at every stage you have to pass some test to advance to the next stage. If you meet someone at a luncheon, at your kid's soccer game, on an airplane or whatever, you must persuade them to let you pass to the next level. For example, maybe their brother-in-law owns a business and is right now thinking about firing an employee for some reason and is quietly searching for a replacement. Why would they pass that juicy tidbit about their brother-in-law's company to you? Stop and think about it for a moment. Would they tell you because you really need a job and they feel sorry for you? Perhaps. Because you're likable? Perhaps. Because they size you up and realize that you just might be someone who can solve their brother-in-law's problem? Perhaps. They will not make a connection on your behalf for no reason. They might know other people who need jobs as well. Every aspect of your interaction with them is contributing to their judgment about whether to give you their brother-in-law's phone number. You must be aware of this when you are networking for a job. You are always interviewing, with everyone that you chitchat with at the school play, sit across from at the community pancake breakfast or make small talk with in the airport bar. You need to be conscious of "your story" and the impression that you make. Ask yourself whether you are successfully promoting those in your human interactions, however casual. I have seen chance encounters lead to interviews because a good impression was made. It led to the job seeker getting forwarded or recommended to an employer who was looking for a certain kind of person. This may look like luck, but as the old saying goes, luck is where preparation and opportunity meet: someone who can tell their story and make a positive impression whenever and wherever they need to is ready for any opportunity that comes their way.

A last thought about networking for a job: do you have a clear idea of what you bring to the table for a potential employer? Someone whose only message is that they are an out-of-work engineer who desperately needs a job is less likely to get a hot tip or be forwarded to another contact than someone who can articulate the problems that they can solve for a potential employer. Know your story, your accomplishments and how to present them, and be ready to do so at all times.

Chapter 12:

Resumes

An *in demand person's* resume isn't, in the end, about them. If you want to be in demand you need to shift the focus of your resume so it's less about you.

If you've read this book this far then you can probably guess what your resume should be about: the employer's problems and how you are the solution they've been looking for. Your resume is not about how you are the person that they've been looking for their whole life (you aren't). It is about how you are a solution, but not a generic solution. It shouldn't be a list of offices or shops that you've worked in for the last twenty years. You need to be a specific solution to a specific problem that they have. Here's a hard fact: the potential employer doesn't care about you: not at all, not even a little bit. I guarantee that when the employer is sifting through a pile of resumes, they have only one thing on their mind: how are they going to get that job done, that problem solved? "The woman who did all the materials purchasing just left to have a baby: now who's going to deal with the suppliers? We're not going to last two weeks without someone getting on top of that situation!" They flip through resumes, spending less than ten seconds scanning each one, looking for a match, like you would rummage through your toolbox looking for the right screwdriver. They aren't looking at you as a whole person, they aren't contemplating the complex and wonderful drama that has been your life, they don't care about your high school swim meets or that you love to bake or paint watercolor landscapes. At that moment they want to find someone so that they can use them. The more you appear to be a specific and useful solution to their problem, the more likely that they'll want to interview you to learn more.

When you write your resume, try to see it through the prospective employer's eyes. You must tell the story of your career as it relates to them, not to your own self-esteem (healthy or fragile as that may be). Your resume is a marketing tool whose only purpose is to get you an interview. It is not your memoirs, your career file or that "permanent record" that you were warned about in high school. Think of it as a television commercial or a magazine ad that's supposed to stimulate a response in someone who sees it. The desired response is to move your resume into the "Call Back for an Interview" pile on a hiring manager's desk. You need to intrigue and even tease the reader into wanting to know more about you. When it comes to resumes, less is more.

So what should the content of your resume be? As we've said over and over, what employers are looking for is someone who can solve their problems. The best predictor of future success is past success, so the best way to convince an employer that you will be a problem-solver is to demonstrate that you have solved problems in the past.

It's astounding how often people misunderstand this, believing that seniority or "experience" counts. I see resumes that proudly assert that the candidate has spent twenty-something years in a position. Big deal. In a booming economy or a seniority culture, maybe that counts for something, but all it tells a prospective employer in a tight economy is that you managed not to get fired for two decades. The employer wonders: Is this someone that will solve my problem or someone that will plant their rear-end, not offend anyone and not break any major rules? Again, big deal. With the company struggling to turn a profit, will this person be a competitive advantage? Will they solve problems or blend into the wallpaper?

Sometimes I see resumes that brag about "experience," measured as having visited a lot of clients, attended a lot of industry conferences and having sat on numerous committees. So what? This is probably a candidate whose career has consisted of being an insider, a knowledgeable gadfly and part of the company's overhead. What reason would a hiring manager have to think that someone like this will be a problem-solver or a competitive advantage for his boss, his department or the company in general? In prosperous times, when companies are making money by the fistful, a company can afford people like this who grease wheels, give advice or sit in meetings that their boss doesn't want to attend. When organizations are throwing out everything but the kitchen sink, these kinds of employees are the first to go. Often they don't understand why, since they were so "experienced."

Your resume must stress accomplishments, and you need

to review your career to understand and explain how in every position that you ever held you solved problems and brought advantages to your employer. Granted, some job types make it easier to quantify accomplishment: a salesperson can talk about meeting or exceeding quotas and a manufacturing manager can brag about having increased productivity. Yet if you think it through, in every position you can explain what you did as meeting a series of challenges. Were you an administrative assistant? Perhaps you could mention how you helped two managers and their staff achieve three major product launches in two years. Did you work in shipping? Perhaps you could explain how you found ways to maintain fulfillment levels through the consolidation of two facilities into one while transitioning to a new software tracking system. Do you get the idea? Look at your previous experience not as time spent on the job but as meeting a series of challenges.

Even the education portion of your resume can and should be accomplishment, rather than experience, driven. Did you go to college for four years? Good for you. Did you do a senior project finding some new way to organize data or teach students using computers? That kind of problem solving might be good for an employer. Did you go to Brazil for a semester? That sounds like it was probably fun, but it won't get you a job. On the other hand, did you overcome language and cultural barriers while working with a team of other students to organize a clinic in a small Brazilian town on your internship? An employer might see you as someone who could help them organize a department made up of immigrant workers.

A word of warning about listing accomplishments: never try to fake them. I have seen people list degrees or skills that they didn't have, make up positions that they didn't hold and list awards that they didn't win. I have seen people get caught in some real whoppers of a lie when an employer ran a background check. More companies are taking the time to investigate backgrounds and resume claims, which is easy to do with the Internet. You run the risk of being terminated or having your offer revoked if you've been dishonest with fabrications, embellishments or omissions. It's better to be honest up front and live with the consequences. I have had candidates boast that they could speak French, Spanish or German on their resume. Please understand: two semesters of college French ten years ago where you learned to count to ten, the major colors and a smattering of travel phrases is not language proficiency. I have seen some of these folks badly embarrassed when the interview begins and the interviewer begins to fluently ask questions in the language claimed on the resume. When the candidate didn't respond in kind, the interview was over.

No matter what accomplishments and skills you list on your resume, they can all be undone by a phenomenon of modern life that might be called the "Anti-Resume." In the chapter on networking I talked about the advantages—or at least what we can learn—from social networking websites like Facebook or MySpace. Facebook, Twitter, or MySpace has completely undermined too many people's resumes, particularly young workers. They might not even realize that it's happening: they just can't understand why they don't get called for interviews. Yet in one recent survey almost a quarter of employers admitted (and surely more just wouldn't admit) that they search for applicants' personal websites. Once something is out on the web, it's in the public domain and there is nothing to prevent a hiring manager from simply typing an applicant's name into a search engine. If they find pages that indicate that the candidate has a character, personality or lifestyle that contradicts the impression which they have created with their resume, then the odds of getting an interview fall quickly. While some might argue that an applicant's personal life should have no bearing on the employment process, the reality is that it does. Candidates who portray themselves as responsible, sober and respectful during the application process but have put material on the Internet that contradicts that impression should not be surprised when the employer chooses not to interview them. There is no reasonable expectation of privacy on the Internet, and all of us should think long and hard about our online "trail." Remember that major search engines store pages, so that even if you pull something down it will leave a sort of fossilized record which could haunt you for years to come.

Almost all of us have had setbacks in our careers, or even outright failures. Some of us didn't hit our numbers and got passed over for promotions or even fired. Some of us lost jobs because we weren't really suited for a job type, a position or a company. Some us didn't get along with a boss and lost our job over it. Some of us screwed up, made bad judgment calls and were terminated for cause over it.

Some of us may have done something even worse: we did

something unethical, dishonest or abusive, got caught and it has haunted us ever since. I know someone who got caught embezzling from a company, was fired and prosecuted for it. She has tried to rebuild a career for years, but understandably employers won't put her in a position of any responsibility and she has worked a series of temporary labor jobs for years. How can she spin something like this on her resume so that she can get back into some sort of management position?

She can't, and neither should you. The first rule of resumes is to be honest, for two good reasons. First, because it's the right thing to do. I'm not going to even waste time explaining why dishonesty is wrong: if you don't get it, I can't explain it. Second, because the odds of getting caught in a lie keep growing with technology. There is so much information out there, and so many ways to gather it, that if you've got skeletons in your closet, you run a genuine risk of them falling out. Confidentiality won't protect you. You'll never hear about it if backchannel industry gossip torpedoes your resume: you just won't get callbacks for interviews. When there are many more applicants than open positions, an employer doesn't need too much justification for selecting other candidates.

You are better off being honest, confronting your past, and working around it. In some cases you will be able to overcome it: if you can solve a problem that a manager has, you may be worth the risk. They have life experience (that's why they are managers) and they know that sometimes a salesperson wasn't a good fit with a product or territory in a past position, but if the candidate can show that they've learned something and bring the right skills to a new position, they can be effective. They know that sometimes personality conflicts can cost someone a job, but if they display energy, enthusiasm and seem like a good match for the new position it might be worth the risk to hire them anyway. People can change, and sometimes people who have been through difficult circumstances and have learned from them might be more useful than someone who hasn't graduated from the school of hard knocks. The burden is going to be on you to show the potential employer why your past failures have made you more useful, not less.

On the other hand, sometimes you just have to accept the consequences of your actions and adjust your career goals. If you embezzled from a former employer or abused a subordinate, it's unlikely that anyone is ever going to give you a position where you can do those things again. You may need to truly reexamine your life and work and retrain yourself for other jobs where you can have the opportunity to succeed.

Make your resume the right length for the position for which you're applying. It doesn't need to chronologically list everything that you have done since ninth grade. It doesn't need to describe every function that you performed within every job that you ever had. It doesn't need to describe your personal life or accomplishments, your marital status, race, religion or likes and dislikes.

That being said, let's talk about the obsession people have with the number of pages that a resume is supposed to be. I hear about this all the time from people who read that a resume should never be more than two pages long. Remember that the hiring manager wants to get as much information about you as possible with as little effort as possible. A four page document with no employment dates and long paragraphs describing the complex details of everything that you ever did requires too much effort. Some people, in a bizarre response to having heard that a resume must never be longer than two pages, simply use a smaller font and shrink the margins, making it even harder for the hiring manager to read. Always think about it from the employer's point of view. Which would you rather receive: a well-written, attractively composed document in a 12-point font that runs three pages or a rambling, incoherent mess that's been squeezed onto two pages with an 8-point font and quarter-inch margins?

The issue isn't really about two pages versus three, or one versus two. The core issue is whether or not you have a concisely written document that provides the right amount of relevant information. If you're 23 years old, straight out of school perhaps, and applying for your first or second job, it's hard to see that you have enough content to go past one page. You may be a superstar: first in your class from Harvard University, you speak Chinese, did an internship with the CEO of Boeing and you wrote a novel when you were 18 years old. That's impressive, will definitely get you interviews, but it also will fit on a single page. On the other hand, perhaps you're a fifty-something executive who has held a series of positions in several industries over the years, has some specialized training and published a series of professional journal articles throughout your career. Three pages might be entirely appropriate to share the pertinent details. Unless you're running for President of the United States you don't need four pages for your resume (and even then you probably don't). Remember, less is more: you want them to bring you in for an interview to learn more.

A poorly written resume invalidates all the supposed accomplishments that you list. It cannot have misspelled words: not one, not ever. It cannot have poor or misused grammar, incorrect parts of speech or verb tenses that don't agree with the subject or object. If you don't know what those things are, get help in writing it from someone who does. Even if you're a professional writer get someone to proofread it. I miss things in my manuscripts all the time. I always have someone, sometimes two people, proofread everything that I write before sending it to be published.

It is the content and quality of the writing that matters, especially in industries where resumes are being submitted electronically. Depending on the type of job, industry or employer, you may not be asked to submit a hard copy of your resume. Some companies or employment services won't accept a hard copy because they can't be easily stored and forwarded around the company. What they will probably want is a word-processing file, most likely in Microsoft Word or PDF format. In those cases the same guidance applies: create an attractive and professional document. Often a manager will have your resume forwarded to them as an email attachment from the Human Resources office and they may print it out so that it's easier to read or make notes on. You may see your document, with all its formatted glory or shame, sitting on a hiring manager's desk during an interview, printed on plain white copy paper, highlighted and underlined with her handwriting scribbled in the margins. So make sure the margins are big enough, the font not too small, and the writing crisp.

Some companies and placement agencies will ask you to enter your resume into an online form. Formatting won't matter at all since you'll be copying and pasting your content into boxes as plain text. One box might ask for education or employment history, another might ask for accomplishments or specialized skills. If you have no artistic touch for fonts and layout then you aren't penalized, but those who do cannot hide behind cosmetics. It comes down to content and writing quality, which must be excellent. Can I say it enough?

A well-written resume has specific characteristics that set it apart from all the others on the manager's desk or in the computer system. It clearly and crisply defines your career; it is easy to read and glean information from. It is accomplishment oriented and value driven. It is to the point and easy to read. It is written in the third person, meaning that it doesn't use the words "I," "me," "we," "they," "us," etc. It will use a lot of verbs and very few adjectives. Its sentences will be declarative and written in the active voice. If you don't know what any of that means, get help. If you don't have the writing skills to put it together, find someone who does.

The story of your career that you tell on your resume is

perhaps your primary tool in your job search. It can open doors: I have seen candidates be given extraordinary interview opportunities because their story was so compelling and well-told. It can also cause doors to be slammed shut. In Demand People have resumes that convince employers they might be the solution to their problems, and that they should be called in for an interview.

Chapter 13:
Interviews

I want to suggest something that might surprise you in a book about career development: job interviews are not sales presentations. The purpose is not to go in and be whatever they want you to be, to schmooze your way into a job by laughing at lame jokes or shoveling insincere praise on the boss's bowling trophy. Yes, you need a job but you are not there to lie, manipulate, seduce or prostitute yourself for that job. You are not there to win the position at all costs.

People who are in demand don't push themselves on others, they discover problems they can solve and opportunities they can develop.

An interview is a discovery process. Both the employer and you have the same goal: to discover if you really are the solution to their problem. If you aren't, no matter how much you need that paycheck, it will end badly for both you and the employer. Think of it from their point of view. Right now they have a problem. They hire you because they think that you're the solution. Maybe that's because they didn't work hard enough to find out if you really are the solution, or because you were slick enough to convince them that you are when you aren't. Regardless, let's say that you get the job. Now one problem has grown to two: the original one and you. You have become a new problem to the company because you're the wrong person for that position. That's bad for them and for you. Sure, you get a paycheck for a while. When a round peg is jammed into a square hole neither the peg nor the hole are going to be happy.

Maybe you're in a chapter in your life when you'd be thrilled to get any paycheck, regardless of whether the job is a perfect fit or not. I understand, and I'm not saying that the interview process is like looking for a soulmate, in which yours and the interviewer's eyes meet and you both know that this was a match made in heaven. What I'm saying is that if you see the interview process as nothing more than a sale to be made, then you will run three risks. First, you can feel defeated when you can't "close a deal." Second, you run the risk of offending the interviewer with what might come off as an insincere or aggressive manner. Third, you might succeed in making a bad match, which will give you a paycheck for a little while but result in wasting months and furthering damaging your resume when, inevitably, you don't work out in the new position.

That doesn't mean that there is no selling going on during the interview. Both you and the company are presenting yourselves as positively as possible in the hope that both of you will discover a mutually beneficial match. Exhibiting basic business manners, courtesy and people skills are not just a technique for making a sale. Those are the things that we owe each other out of simple respect. They are the obligations of civilization. If you only switch on manners, courtesy and decent people skills when you're trying to "sell," then I assume that most of the time you are rude and inconsiderate. I hope that you don't get a job with my organization, because I don't want to have to work with you every day after you've "closed the deal" with the hiring manager. As a manager, whenever I've considered hiring someone, I've always been turned off if I feel that I'm being "sold." I wonder what they'll become after I've bought them. That's what I want to discover as a manager before I hire them.

Instead of thinking of the interview as a sales presentation, I'd like for you to think of it as a blind date. Both of you have heard about the other, and now it's time to meet to see if what intrigued both of you on paper leads to personal chemistry. Be yourself (your best self), but be yourself. Learn as much as you share, to discover if you're interested in pursuing this. Find out where it goes. If it's working, great. If it's not, you can't make it work.

There are some mechanics to the interview process. There are questions that you should be prepared to answer and to ask, and if you haven't thought them through in advance, then you are simply unprepared. There are topics that you should try to steer the conversation toward and some that you should absolutely avoid. There are specific cultural cues that you should both give and look for. There are cultural rituals and best practices.

For example, there is absolutely no excuse for not

preparing for the interview. If an employer calls you into an interview and you can't make the time or effort to prepare, then honestly, you don't deserve the job. You should try and know as much about the company as possible. You can act interested in the company during the interview, and you might even get away with it. You can be genuinely interested and not have to fake it. How do you show genuine interest to the interviewer? Research the company before going in. Throughout my years in the recruiting industry I've noticed that one characteristic of people who ace their interviews and get offers is that they come into the company already knowing as much as, or in some cases more, about the business than the person conducting the interview.

Your interview isn't a quiz show, nor is it an interview in the way that a newspaper reporter asking a celebrity questions is an interview. Your interview should be a first meeting between you and the people that you hope to work for. It should be a conversation, a constructive give-and-take in which you ask as many questions as you answer. This is what I meant by a "process of discovery," as both sides try to find out if the two of you are a good match. I will often ask someone after an interview if they had found out exactly what they would do, who they would work for or how much travel would be involved. Too many times I have and been told, "I'm not sure, we didn't really talk about that." If so, then it was a missed opportunity for that person to discover whether the job would be a good fit for them. If they do get an offer it might answer some of their questions, especially the compensation, but an offer letter or phone call is unlikely to give them all the information they need to make a well-informed decision. They had that opportunity in the interview and they didn't take it. You should go into an interview with a list of questions that you need to get answered and tactfully work through them. If the company is unable or unwilling to tell you want you need to know to be able to commit yourself to their team it might be a sign that you won't ever feel comfortable there.

When you can be conversational in the interview it demonstrates to the interviewer that you can work with others. If you are passive and only answer direct questions while nodding your head occasionally, you won't give the impression that you will be able to engage and participate as a member of a team. The interviewer might wonder if this is your normal mode in meetings and over the phone: when working with other employees or customers will you ask questions if you need more information? Will you be passive and not voluntarily contribute to the group's knowledge? They are trying to discover who you are, not play Twenty Questions or dig responses out of you. If you can put the interviewer at ease, engage in an easy and productive conversation in that setting, it's a good indication of what type of employee you might be.

If the interview is a discovery process, a sort of "first date," then you should also be prepared to discover that it isn't a good match. Certainly the employer is prepared to discover through the interview that you aren't the person they are looking for. Yet the unemployed person often feels so desperate for a job, any job, that they haven't considered the possibility that during the interview they might discover that this job would be wrong for them. When the conversation is going badly the candidate's temptation is to start trying to please the interviewer, saying whatever they think will win the job for them.

Here's a hard truth: sometimes the wrong job is worse than no job at all. You might get a paycheck, for a little while, until it becomes apparent to both parties that it isn't working out. In the meantime you might make yourself and everyone around you miserable, waste weeks or months that could have been spent looking for the right job and put a failure as the most recently held slot on your resume. Walking away can be a sign of either immaturity or maturity, depending on your motivations. I'm not talking about turning your nose up because you think that the position is beneath you or storming off in a snit because you don't get everything that you think you want or deserve. I'm talking about having the self-awareness to know when something will not be right for you and the confidence to keep looking for another job rather than put yourself in a situation where you cannot succeed or be happy.

There are things that I shouldn't have to say because they are obvious, yet I see people ignore them constantly. For example, dress appropriately for the situation. I once had a candidate, a very bright engineer, who dressed and groomed himself like someone going to a Halloween party as a "nerd." His weirdly out–of-fashion clothes and "Prince Valiant" haircut turned heads whenever he walked into an office for an interview. He couldn't understand why he wasn't getting callbacks or offers, considering his accomplishments. After all, wouldn't he be able to solve the company's technical problems? What he failed to understand was that the way he presented himself made managers fear that while he might offer technical solutions, he also might create people problems. Most positions in modern companies, even in engineering departments, involve teamwork and interpersonal communication. I certainly didn't want him to sell himself insincerely, but I saw no reason for him to handicap himself in the interview process. I asked him to trust me and sent him to a local men's clothing shop that I had a relationship with and then to a barber I knew. With a new suit and a haircut, his next interview resulted in an offer.

Does this contradict my earlier point about not pretending to be someone that you are not? What happens when, a couple of days into the job, a guy like that goes back to wearing his own clothes and growing his hair back out? If that happens, then he didn't use the interview as an opportunity for him to discover what the company's values and culture were. My goal in getting him a suit and a haircut was not just to clean him up for the hiring manager; it was to teach him something. Hopefully, he learned about what it took to be a part of the company, namely that beyond having technical expertise, the employees there dressed and groomed sharply. That interview was his opportunity to discover whether they were a good fit for him, not just the other way around. If he felt uncomfortable with their culture during the interview then he shouldn't have taken the offer. He would never have learned that, if he hadn't presented himself positively enough to go in and engage in the interview process.

By far, the most important factor in presenting yourself

positively is passion and energy. There are simple truths about human interaction, and one of them is that people respond to the energy level of the person that they are speaking with. If your voice and demeanor are positive and upbeat, if you project a serious purpose with a light heart and a twinkle in your eye, most people are going to adjust their energy level to match yours. Again, I am not telling you to adopt an insincere tone in an attempt to sell a false image of yourself. What I am saying is that the employer is discovering who you are during the interview, and you want them to see the best of your energy and attitude on display. Not something fake or contrived, but not you at your most passive and tentative, either.

If we invite someone to visit our home, common sense and common courtesy indicates that we should pick the newspapers up off the floor and not answer the door in our underwear and slippers. Common sense and common courtesy are the basic grease that allows people to work together. Displaying sense and courtesy in how you dress, speak and behave at an interview isn't selling, it's allowing the employer to discover that you have those qualities and that you would probably make use of them if you came to work in their business.

What I'm arguing for can be summed up as integrity: being honest about who you are and showing sincere respect and interest in the employer. Integrity in an interview means that you value yourself and the employer enough to show respect for the occasion. It also means that you are genuinely curious about the employer and what they have to say, and not dominating the time with a "sales pitch" about yourself. It means not groping for superficial connections with the interviewer or showering them with meaningless compliments. Integrity in an interview means engaging in the process without allowing desperation or any other extreme emotions to control your thoughts, voice or mannerisms. It means both answering and asking questions fairly. If you present yourself as a positive and polite person, a problem solver with energy, passion and integrity, you will stand out among the candidates being interviewed for any job, no matter how many there are.

Section IV:
"Manage Your Career"

Chapter 14:
Forever Young

Youth is wasted on the young. It's one of my favorite sayings.

Have you ever daydreamed about how you would do things differently if you could go back to high school and start over? The older you get, the more you speculate about stuff like that, because you realize that young people have so many opportunities and so much potential. They have years ahead of them to accomplish things and so many options that they can apply themselves to. They have few obligations, plenty of energy and they learn things more quickly.

Young people don't realize how good they have it, which is where the saying above comes in. They don't have the life-experience to know how to develop their potential, and they often squander time and opportunities because they think that those things are in endless supply. As we get older we can't help but think that if we had all that energy and possibility again, and we could apply what we've learned through the school of hard knocks, we'd do a better job at life the second time around.

We can't, of course.

While we can't be young again, what if we could live and learn like we were? What if we could be more flexible and fearless? What if we could pick up new technologies and techniques easily? What if we were more willing to start and build things? What if we didn't project an air of seniority-based entitlement? If we could act like that, but mix in some of our experience and discernment, we might be more in demand as an employee or contractor.

For the reasons we'll talk about in this chapter, I think that we have to learn to be forever young in attitude, aptitude and adaptability. If we don't, the cost of our skills and services (I'll explain what I mean by that in a minute) is going to rise and the demand for them is going to fall.

One of the more obvious reasons for this is the pace of technological change. New products, services and methods used to evolve on a scale of decades. Decades became years and are rapidly becoming months. Moore's Law is a famous axiom of the computer industry, observing that the computing power of hardware doubles about every two years. Web-based technologies are changing how we work and interact with each other at an equally blistering pace. Consider social networking: Facebook was rolled out to the general public in September of 2006, but by the end of 2009 more than 300 million people around the world were using it to communicate and network in an entirely new way. Consider smart phones: every day new iPhone and Droid phone applications are coming out which change the way people work, shop and interact with each other.

These are simple and benign examples, but the point is serious. Younger people pick this stuff up quickly and are able to adapt rapidly because they're less cognitively invested in existing technology or techniques. Of course part of the foolishness of youth is to run after new fads, and some of us who are older tell ourselves that we don't need every newfangled gadget and gizmo. We fool ourselves if we don't recognize that some changes are genies that will never go back into the bottle.

In a highly developed economy, profits come and go quickly, based on information, speed and the ability to adapt to the demands of customers. To compete, businesses need to be able to shift models and methods on a dime. Employees that can't keep up are liabilities, not assets. That sounds cold and cruel, but it's true.

Wayne Gretzy is the all-time leading scorer in professional hockey. He had an uncanny ability to be in the right place on the ice at the right time to set himself up to score. When asked how, he has repeatedly said that other players saw the puck and skated toward it, while he anticipated where it was going and got there first. Whether you work for yourself or others, you need to be able to figure out the demands of your job before you become obsolete. Again, that sounds cruel, because we want to believe that a faithful business or employee has earned enough loyalty through years of service to be able to rest a bit on their laurels. That's just not the way it works in a fast moving, global and digital economy.

Let's talk about money. If you've ever run a business you know that your labor cost is overhead. I don't care if you sell hot dogs from a cart by the subway station, what you pay yourself gets deducted from the what you collect from every dog.

There used to be a pattern, especially in union-driven industries and big organizations: the longer you worked the more money you got paid, based on nothing more than seniority. Your overhead went up not because you brought in more revenue or increased profit, but just because you had been around long enough to deserve a bigger slice of the pie. There are at least four problems with that approach in today's economy.

First, the whole premise of that model is that your pay is about your needs, not the employer's or the customer's. I know that we rationalized it by saying that seniority added to the organization in some undefined way, with older workers sharing their wisdom and experience. In practice, however, the idea of seniority was usually about the needs of the worker: they had bigger house payments, kids in college, retirement looming, etc. As I've said over and over, people hire or buy things to solve their problems, not the problems of the employee or seller. If you can't solve their problem any better than someone who is twenty years younger (who doesn't have kids in college, etc.), then they aren't going to pay any more for your wages or services or products. I know: it's unfair, heartless, cruel, etc. I'll bet you that you aren't any different when you're the consumer: if there are two hot dog carts on the corner you won't pay a dollar more for a Chicago dog from Cart A because the owner is older and more experienced. Cart B's dog is the same, or good enough, and a dollar less. Welcome to the marketplace. Welcome to Earth.

Therefore, one of the challenges as we get older is to not paint ourselves into a corner with overhead and expectations. I remember (and plenty of people my age will say this) that some of the happiest years my wife and I have known were when we were young and starting our careers. Sure, at the time we were frustrated because we wanted to make more money, but we had freedom that we've lost as we made, bought and obligated ourselves to more stuff. When we were young we could take new jobs, relocate and live on less. In many ways we were happier. Life was an adventure. Being "forever young" means staying adventurous.

Second, a rapid-paced technological society is less likely to sustain a career path premised on seniority. Consider this book. My co-author and his colleagues used to send edited manuscripts to a gentleman who owned a typesetting business. He had decades of experience, receiving countless manuscripts from editors and then expertly preparing them to be sent to the printers. His sons and their wives worked in the business with him, and their family had a great reputation as the ideal old-style craftsman with apprentice children who were learning to carry on the family tradition.

Then came software. At first it was expensive and hard to use. It was more of a tool for craftsmen who still understood the typesetting business. This gentleman bought it, his sons learned it, and they continued to do their work with it. Then the software became consumer-based. Anyone could buy it for a few hundred dollars and install it on a business-priced computer. Then it got even less expensive, and would run on any consumer computer you bought from a big-box store. It's not fair to say that anyone can typeset a book, but anyone who learns and experiments a few times can do a book like this one. It might not be done as expertly as the old craftsmen and his sons, but it's good enough and costs a fraction of what the old typesetter charged.

Now consumers are starting to download digital books. Those files can be prepared in just a few hours with a word processor and basic knowledge of website coding.

Technology is moving so quickly that old notions of charging for experience and seniority are becoming harder to sustain. That's bad news if you're an old guy who wants to charge for those things, good news if you're an entrepreneur who's looking for ways to get things done faster and cheaper.

Does that mean that quality has to suffer? It depends on what you produce. Because it's so easy to produce books today the emphasis is more on the content. It means that good writers can focus on their writing, and that less time and money is wrapped up in the mechanics of production.

Third, seniority is a hard concept to sustain in a globalized economy. Outsourcing, web-based solutions and migration means that we have to compete in bigger pools. It's harder to protect jobs and get paid more when consumers have other options.

Finally, demographics are working against the idea of older workers being protected and paid more just because they're older. As the workforce ages, the organizational pyramid is getting flipped upside-down. It used to be that a few older folks were at the top, getting paid more than the young people at the base, because of the scarcity of their age and experience. What happens when there are more older people—all with experience and seniority—and a smaller number of young people? Especially if those younger workers are willing to do more, and relocate if necessary, for less money? The laws of supply and demand dictate that the younger, cheaper, more flexible workers will be more in demand than legions of older workers who want to preserve their perks. We can complain about this state of affairs, but what can we do about it? The baby boomers didn't have enough kids to sustain their generational perks as they aged.

We can get angry about this state of affairs. I suppose that one of the perks of being an older guy like me is to think that the world is going to hell in a hand basket. While we can grumble, we can't do much to change it.

The alternative is to change ourselves. Instead of being grumbling older folks (or instead becoming that, for those of you who are young now) we can have a youthful attitude, keep our minds open and our skills sharp.

What does that mean in your particular job or business?

It's hard to say, but I'm certain that it's always better to approach your work with a curious, competitive and adventurous spirit than to feel entitled, defensive and angry. I'm also certain that it makes you more in demand, as well.

Chapter 15:
Live Within Your Means

The United States was founded on the rationale that you are endowed by your Creator with certain unalienable Rights, that among these are life, liberty and the pursuit of happiness. The stated purpose of our government is to secure these rights. That means that you have a right to be free, and that your government is accountable to guarantee your freedom. The promise of freedom, of the opportunity to be and become whomever you want to be, has brought waves of immigrants to these shores for two centuries.

We can debate all day long about how this or that government policy limits our freedom, but one thing is beyond argument: you can give away your liberty and opportunity. Too many Americans have frittered away their freedom through indebtedness. Debt steals possibility from your future. We no longer toss debtors into prison, but many of us are living in a prison of our own making. It is a gilded cage: a couple of really cool cars or trucks, granite counter tops in the kitchen, a closet full shoes "that are to die for". The availability of easy credit, starting right out of high school, leads to lives of indentured service: not to a merchant or farmer but to banks and mortgage companies. Too many people can never become what they want to be because they are shackled to paying for what they are.

In Demand People are oriented toward solving problems and developing opportunities. It's difficult to be focused on serving your employers or customers when you are staggering under large consumer debts while living paycheck to paycheck.

You have the right, as an American, to be free from self-imposed debt. You may have become overly dependent on your job. Don't get me wrong, I'm not saying that you don't need to work for money. I'm not telling you to move to a cabin in the woods, wear animal skins and grow your own turnips. Nor am I suggesting that we all should work for low-paying non-profits or go overseas and be missionaries. Many of us, maybe even you, might want to change jobs for a variety of reasons: location, vocation, to take a risk to advance or to downsize and go back to school, to start a business, whatever. If we are tied to an overvalued house and a pile of consumer debt, we can't afford to risk our direct-deposit paychecks. The irony is that the more risks we take with our spending, the less risks we can take with our work.

In Demand People don't expect other people, including the government, to bail them out. When they look at those words in the Declaration of Independence they don't see an entitlement to push their debt onto other people. They preserve their liberty and don't try to steal some freedom from neighbors who more wisely preserved theirs.

In Demand People have the freedom to develop their career or business without burdens or bailouts. You can have that kind of liberty as well. How? It's simple: don't spend more than you make. Live below your means, not above or even right at them. Start getting rid of your debt as fast as possible and avoid any new debt like a coiled rattlesnake in the corner of your tent. There are times and reasons to borrow money, but they should be few and far between. This is not a debt management or financial planning book, but get one and start following its advice.

Living below your means instead of above, makes it possible for you to take a lower paying job because it's more interesting to you, is in a better location or offers the possibility to advance down the line, etc. It makes starting your own business more feasible. It allows you to consider career changes or short-term work projects as a subcontractor. It certainly makes it easier to survive through economic cycles. I'm not suggesting that you curtail your ambitions at all: if you dream of making a million dollars a year, then just plan to live on half a million (that shouldn't be too tough). If you make fifty grand, can you live on forty?

Beyond reducing debt and spending less than you make, you can hold onto your freedom by paying more attention to micro-economies than to macro-economies. Macro-economies are the big cycles: the national and global financial markets, international trade, the fortunes of countries and huge corporations. We may form opinions about these but we have have no direct control over them. By contrast, micro-economies are small networks of commerce and trade. You have much more control over your own micro-economy than you do over global economic cycles. Where will you live and how much will you pay for that? Can you buy a duplex, live in one half and rent the other out to minimize your housing costs? Can you work your life out so that you can walk to work or minimize your commute? Can you negotiate with your employer to be a subcontractor in return for other advantages like working from home? Can your family start a small business? Where will you shop? Can you join or form purchasing cooperatives to negotiate better terms for things that you buy or need? Can you engage in house-swaps for vacations? Will you buy a rental house just to put tenants in it and generate a revenue stream, not to "flip" it for resale? Sure, you'll have to fix toilets and collect rent, but you'll also have more control than you would speculating.

One type of micro-economy that I've mentioned before is bartering networks. You can work out a straight barter arrangement between families to reduce expenses (I'll clean your house if you cut my kid's hair), or factor trade into small business exchanges (my real estate agent will reduce his commission if my web-design business makes improvements in his site). The goal is to take control of whatever you can, wherever you can, to preserve as much freedom as possible so that you can live your life without dependency on employers, financial markets or government.

In 1776 the Continental Congress asked Thomas Jefferson

to write a "declaration of independence." Most of the founders believed that governments should guarantee and guard the idea of private property (whether that's real estate or a comic book collection). In his first draft Jefferson substituted the phrase "pursuit of happiness" for "property" as the third right that the Creator gives and for which governments are implemented to defend.

Government gives you a right to pursue happiness, not to be happy. It is not supposed to even out all our outcomes, to make sure that everyone gets the same rewards in life regardless of talent, choices, opportunity or effort. The genius of America is that it gives you the right to be a fool and a right to fail.

Claim that right to pursue happiness. Do not depend on or expect anyone else to provide your happiness, not employers, financial markets, politicians or government bureaucracies. Heed this warning: if you believe that the government or other institutions exist to give you a right to happiness, to provide it for you, then they will determine what that happiness is. They will hand you whatever it is that they are selling and say, "Here. Be happy with this. Now say, 'Thank you.' It might be government handouts, a government house or a government health plan. It might be a corporation, with all its benefits and perks, that you are trusting to take care of you. Please listen: whoever is guaranteeing your happiness decides what it will be.

Jefferson went out of his way in his first draft of the Declaration of Independence to make the point that the government exists to give you a right to pursue whatever it is that you decide will make you happy. That might be inventing the Next Greatest Thing or playing with it. It might be making a fortune or living like a hobo, raising a family in the suburbs or performing as a street mime in Times Square. You get to choose and you get to assume the rights and risks of that pursuit. If you give away your right to fail you will give away your right to succeed, to pursue happiness as you define it.

I hope that some of you try to launch global corporations from your garage, invent great things or make obscenely large fortunes. I hope that some of you do all the above. Our country and our world desperately need your achievement. I would be remiss if I didn't close this book by reminding you that pursuing money for its own sake has gotten too many of us into trouble. Capitalism is the most effective engine to drive growth and prosperity and justice that history has ever seen, and as the economist Adam Smith said, the profit motive is like an "invisible hand," that guides free markets, creating wealth and opportunity and jobs and all the miracles and wonders of technology.

Hopefully, your passion isn't money for its own sake. I hope that you are motivated to achieve because of the valuable things that you can do with the money you earn. Cheap money, money that you don't really work for, brings very little genuine happiness. Think that's an anti-capitalist statement? Not at all, because many millionaires and billionaires enjoy their money as a happy consequence of a productive life. Contrast that with lottery winners. Too many people who win the big jackpot just blow it, and many end up miserable. It's wealth disconnected from achievement or value: just stuff dumped on someone without the character to appreciate it. The same thing could be said for trust funders at one end of the economic ladder and those who grow up on welfare at the other. Money, just money, disconnected from value, is nothing but trouble. Consider chapter 5, verses 10-11 of the Old Testament Book of Ecclesiastes:

> *Whoever loves money never has money enough; whoever loves wealth is never satisfied with his income. This too is meaningless. As goods increase, so do those who consume them. And what benefit are they to the owner except to feast his eyes on them?*

Pursue happiness. It's your right as an American citizen. Don't depend on anyone else for it, and don't let anyone tell you what it should be. Some of you, in pursuing happiness, will do things so useful to the rest of us that you will make a pile of money. Good for you, but all that money will be the fruit of a happy pursuit, not the object.

Chapter 16:
A Life Worth Living

You probably read this book because you were looking for some way to find a job, develop your career and be more successful. That's what the book cover promised it would be about, and I hope that it's been helpful. Let me end by asking you to reflect about what it means to you to have a "successful" career.

Of course the most obvious thing that comes to mind is financial success. We would all like to be so in demand that employers and customers will pay a high price for our services. If you follow the principles in this book, matched by ability and effort, I believe that you will enjoy financial success. A successful career can mean more than just making money.

There is nothing wrong with working to make money, even with the aim of making a lot of money. It's your responsibility to feed and house and clothe your family, and any work you do for that purpose has dignity. We should never hold out from doing honest labor for an honest buck because we demand that our work be fun or that we find it rewarding or that it comes with sufficient status and perks and security and not too many hours or stress. Being in demand isn't some pie-in-the-sky ideal about how we are entitled to work only on our terms. Work is necessary, it's often hard and it rarely earns us as much money as we want or need. It's often insecure.

Our work is not the same thing as our life. It can contribute to our life or can corrode it, leaving us scarred and weakened. A large part of our lives consists of work but we do not need to waste a very large part of our lives working. What's the difference? It's a matter of how your work is directed.

When you are unemployed or underemployed your need for a better job is always staring you in the face. The broken car that you can't afford to fix, the child's tuition payment that you can't make, the health insurance that you simply can't afford, period. It's easy to become so absorbed in your various efforts that you become self-centered.

I agree that people who are obsessed with scrambling after enough money for all their wants and needs are selfish and intolerant. It almost goes without saying that if you focus exclusively on your own problems you leave no room in your heart, mind or soul for anyone else. Your life is poor. I do not agree that such people are always the unemployed or underemployed or working class or poor. I have known plenty of wealthy people in my life, and even more that want to be wealthy. Some of them had the most self-obsessed and self-absorbed and self directed lives that I've ever seen. The opposite is also true: I've known many rich people who were humble, considerate and generous. I've seen the same contrasts in the poor, the underemployed and the unemployed. I've never seen any correlation between someone's generosity and concern for others and their income. Kind, thoughtful and giving people have lives that reflect that, regardless of whether they make $30,000 or $300,000 per year.

Winston Churchill said, "We make a living by what we get, but we make a life by what we give." Your career can become a long, selfish obsession over your own needs, but it doesn't have to be. It shouldn't be. If your heart is soft and gracious, and if you genuinely care about other people, there is no reason that any of those qualities have to stop while you meet the challenges of developing your career or business.

Your life doesn't have to be a reflection of your circumstances; instead, your circumstances can reflect your life. I'm not saying that you can simply "think and grow rich" or any such nonsense. You can have joy and dignity regardless of how much money you make, where you live or what you do for a living. You can bless the people around you with your words and manners. These are the building blocks of a life worth living, as we've talked about all through this book. While we make a living with our work, we make a worthy life by caring for others, by giving what we can to them, by sharing whatever we have to build a legacy and make the world around us better. You may not be able to cure AIDS or feed the hungry in Africa or donate a new wing to the hospital, but you can have an impact on the lives of people around you. Mother Theresa, who gave her life to serving the poorest of the poor in Calcutta, said, "If you can't feed a hundred people, then just feed one." She also said, "We cannot do great things on this Earth, only small things with great love." That is how you stop working for a living, and start working for a life that is worth living.

I didn't know Jack Klunder, but I would have liked him if I had. I like people with snow on the roof and wisdom in their hearts who aren't afraid to speak their minds. From what I've heard Jack was that kind of guy. I was introduced to "the world according to Jack" when my wife Barb and I were visiting our friend Erin recently at her home. On the wall above Erin's back door is painted "Make Your Mission In Life Someone Other Than Yourself." I read it several times. Then I asked Erin about it and she told me it was her grandfather Jack that said it as he prepared to die. She said that they were all gathered around Jack's bed during his last hours of life when someone asked Grandpa Jack for his wisdom for life. Jack told the family, "Love your spouse with all your heart and make your mission in life someone other than yourself."

In our society we refer to people of age somewhat dismissively as the "elderly" unlike all other cultures on the planet that refer to those that are at the top end of the age spectrum more respectfully as "the elders," a position of respect and veneration. Jack wasn't elderly, he was an elder.

The older I get the more it's confirmed to me that you can have the finest education that money can buy but only life experience gives you wisdom. I've met people with big educations in my more than two decades in the people business.

I never met one of the young ones that could hold a candle to a guy like Jack. That is why if I can give you any kind of advice it's to respect those with life experience and ask them for their guidance. Then do something that will show that you have gained some wisdom in life, follow their advice.

When Jack was asked for his wisdom he gave it. He left them with a challenge, a challenge to be bigger than themselves. Is there anything we can aspire to that is a better goal than to be devoted to something bigger than we are?

Throughout this book I've talked about ways that In Demand People are not self-absorbed or self-serving. They never have a shortage of employers and customers because they focus on solving other people's problems. They spend more time discovering opportunities than thinking about their own ambitions. The paradox is that these qualities benefit them, in the end. They invest in other people and get a huge return for that investment. Employers want to hire them, promote them and keep them. Customers become loyal, and keep on hiring or buying from them. They are rewarded when people compete for their skills and services. The irony of their careers is that they are in demand because they are not demanding.

I get sentimental around Christmas, and look back to see what I accomplished or didn't accomplish that year. I've tried to live out Jack's admonition. For nearly a quarter century my lovely wife Barbara and I have worked hard on behalf of poor children to try to give them a voice and better life. My Christian faith has compelled me to believe that reaching out to children is a noble cause and I can't think of a better way to do it than to sponsor a child through an organization like Compassion International. However you do it, serve something bigger than yourself and someone less fortunate than yourself.

I'm not suggesting that we measure the value of our life by what we gave, or "gave back," or the "legacy" that we left behind. Again, who measures that? Against what standard? Did the philanthropist who built a college library or the businessperson who leaves it all to become a missionary "accomplish" more than the faithful wife who raised decent children and helped her husband keep his business afloat? Did the lives of the heart surgeon who saved thousands, or of the activist who fed the homeless please God more than the man who was kind to his sister, kept his wedding vows and forgave and blessed his father at his deathbed? The "butterfly effect" is the notion that the flapping of a butterfly's wings on the West coast of Africa creates a small turbulence that, through an infinite and complex chain of events, results in a hurricane slamming into Miami. Who measure's what the ultimate value of anything that we do will be?

We may not be able to measure all the outcomes of what we do in this life, but we can control the focus. I subtitled this book *How to Get Hired, Develop a Career and Always be Successful.* If you solve other people's problems, serve other people's needs and develop the opportunities that life gives you-- and if you do all that while speaking well, telling a compelling story about yourself and giving generously to those less fortunate than yourself--then I guarantee that you will always be *in demand* and enjoy more success in your career than you can imagine.

About the Author

For twenty five years Bill Van Steenis has been an executive recruiter, and has matched up hundreds of men and women with companies all around the world. His first book, *The ReExamined Life: Finding a Better Life After Losing a Job,* was released in 2009. He lives with his family in Holland, Michigan.

You can learn more, arrange for him to speak to your group or contact him by visiting *www.reexaminelife.com.*

About the Co-Author

Greg Smith is a writer, teacher and designer. He lives with his family in Holland, Michigan, and is senior partner in Black Lake Studio/Press. You can contact him by visiting *www.blacklakestudio.com.*